M...m...my jaw...hurts...!!! What is this?! It's super-duper painful... Even chewing tofu hurts! Is this what they call TMJD?!

—Masashi Kishimoto, 2013

岸本斉史

Author/artist Masashi Kishimoto was born in 1974 in rural Okayama Prefecture, Japan. After spending time in art college, he won the Hop Step Award for new manga artists with his manga **Karakuri** (Mechanism). Kishimoto decided to base his next story on traditional Japanese culture. His first version of **Naruto**, drawn in 1997, was a one-shot story about fox spirits; his final version, which debuted in **Weekly Shonen Jump** in 1999, quickly became the most popular ninja manga in Japan.

NARUTO VOL. 67
SHONEN JUMP Manga Edition

STORY AND ART BY MASASHI KISHIMOTO

Translation/Mari Morimoto
Touch-up Art & Lettering/John Hunt
Design/Sam Elzway
Editor/Alexis Kirsch

Printed in the U.S.A.

Published by VIZ Media, LLC
P.O. Box 77010
San Francisco, CA 94107

10 9 8 7 6 5 4 3 2 1
First printing, October 2014

www.viz.com

PARENTAL ADVISORY
NARUTO is rated T for Teen and is recommended for ages 13 and up. This volume contains realistic and fantasy violence.
ratings.viz.com

www.shonenjump.com

NARUTO
VOL. 67
AN OPENING
STORY AND ART BY
MASASHI KISHIMOTO

CHARACTERS

Naruto うずまきナルト

Sasuke うちはサスケ

Kakashi はたけカカシ

Sakura 春野サクラ

Sai サイ

Yamato ヤマト

Kurama 九喇嘛

Obito うちはオビト

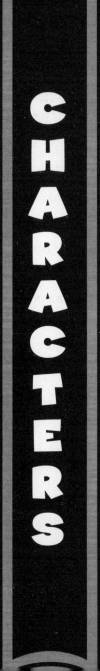

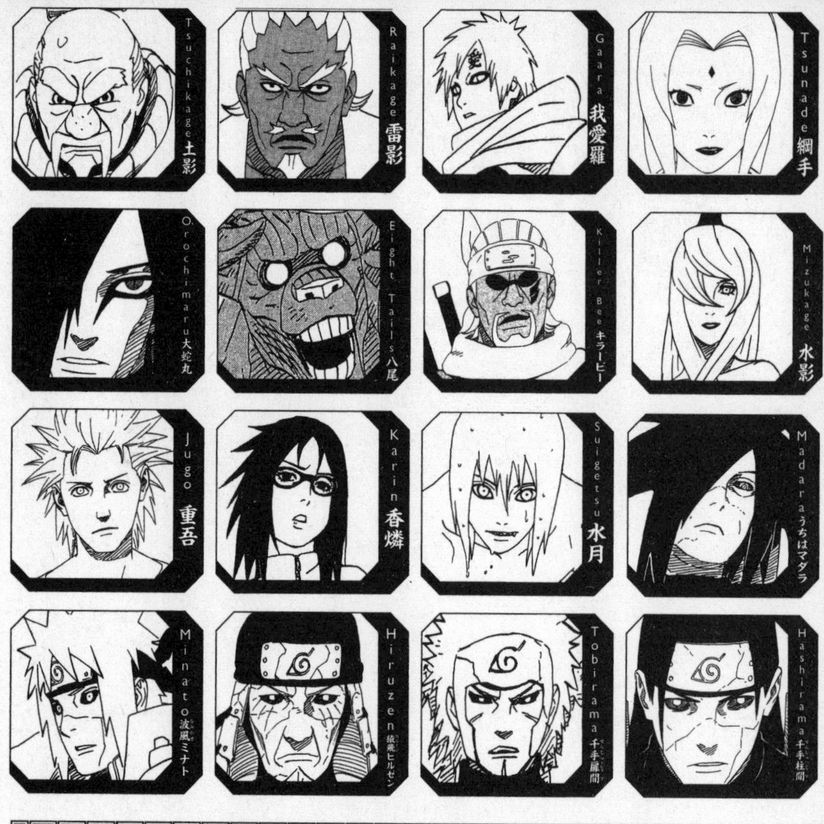

THE STORY SO FAR...

Naruto, the biggest troublemaker at the Ninja Academy in the Village of Konohagakure, finally becomes a ninja along with his classmates Sasuke and Sakura. They grow and mature through countless trials and battles. However, Sasuke, unable to give up his quest for vengeance, leaves Konohagakure to seek Orochimaru and his power…

Two years pass. Naruto grows up and engages in fierce battles against the Tailed Beast-targeting Akatsuki. And the Fourth Great Ninja War against the Akatsuki finally begins. Naruto and his companions face off against the reunited Obito and Madara in order to stop the resurrected Ten Tails! Ten Tails' power seems too great to handle, but Sasuke enters the battlefield along with the Edotensei-resurrected former Hokage. With Cell 7 reunited at last, the battle starts to turn in Naruto's favor. However, Obito then surprises everyone by becoming the Ten Tails' jinchuriki!

NARUTO

VOL. 67

AN OPENING

CONTENTS

GGGGGGG

?!!

Number 638: Ten Tails' Jinchuriki, Obito

!
!
ZWWWW
ZWWW
ZWWW

ZMOO
GRRR...
KRAA
KR
ZMOOOO
OOOO
ZMOOOO

ALL OF TEN TAILS... WAS COMPLETELY ABSORBED... INTO THAT MAN...
ITS CHAKRA TOO.
THEN, ARE YOU SAY-ING...
THOOM
THAT'S THE TEN TAILS'...

...JINCHURIKI?

HE LOOKS EVEN CREEPIER THAN BEFORE.
OBITO...
NARUTO, HOW CAN YOU TELL?!

!!
SHIVER
WH- WHAT IS THIS I FEEL?
MM...
JINCHURIKI, EH. THIS IS BAD.

I'VE BECOME FRIENDS WITH THE OTHER BIJU!
THEY GAVE ME SOME OF THEIR CHAKRA EARLIER, SO IT'S OBVIOUS TO ME!!

I FELT THE BIJU'S CHAKRA GET SUCKED INSIDE OBITO ONE AFTER ANOTHER...
...PLUS I'VE SEEN THAT SIX PATHS REBIRTH JUTSU BEFORE TOO!

HE WAS WEAVING **DIFFERENT** SIGNS!!
I SEE.
ANYWAY, HE WAS PERFORMING THE JUTSU TO BECOME A JINCHURIKI ALL ALONG!

EIGHT-O! IS THAT ITS FINAL FORM?

NO, IT'S NOT.
IT'S DIFFICULT TO EXPLAIN, BUT THAT AIN'T IT.
IT SEEMS TEN TAILS WAS USED TO CREATE A JINCHURIKI BEFORE IT REACHED FINAL FORM.

HMPH !!

WHOOSH

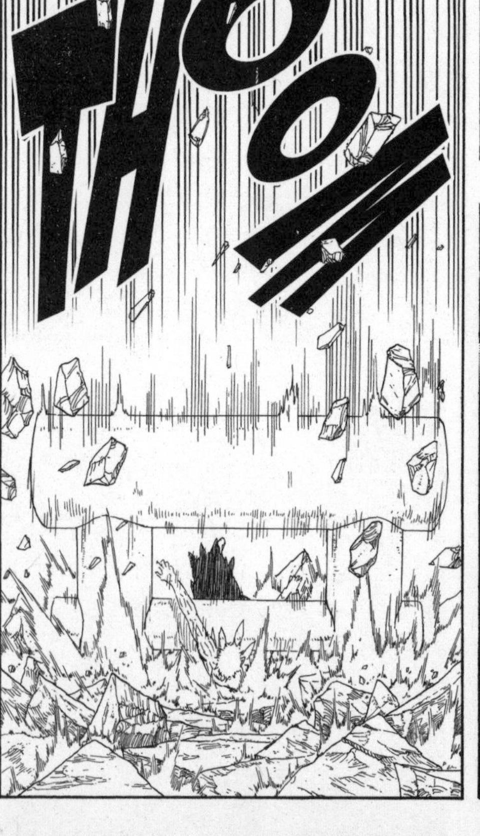
THOOM

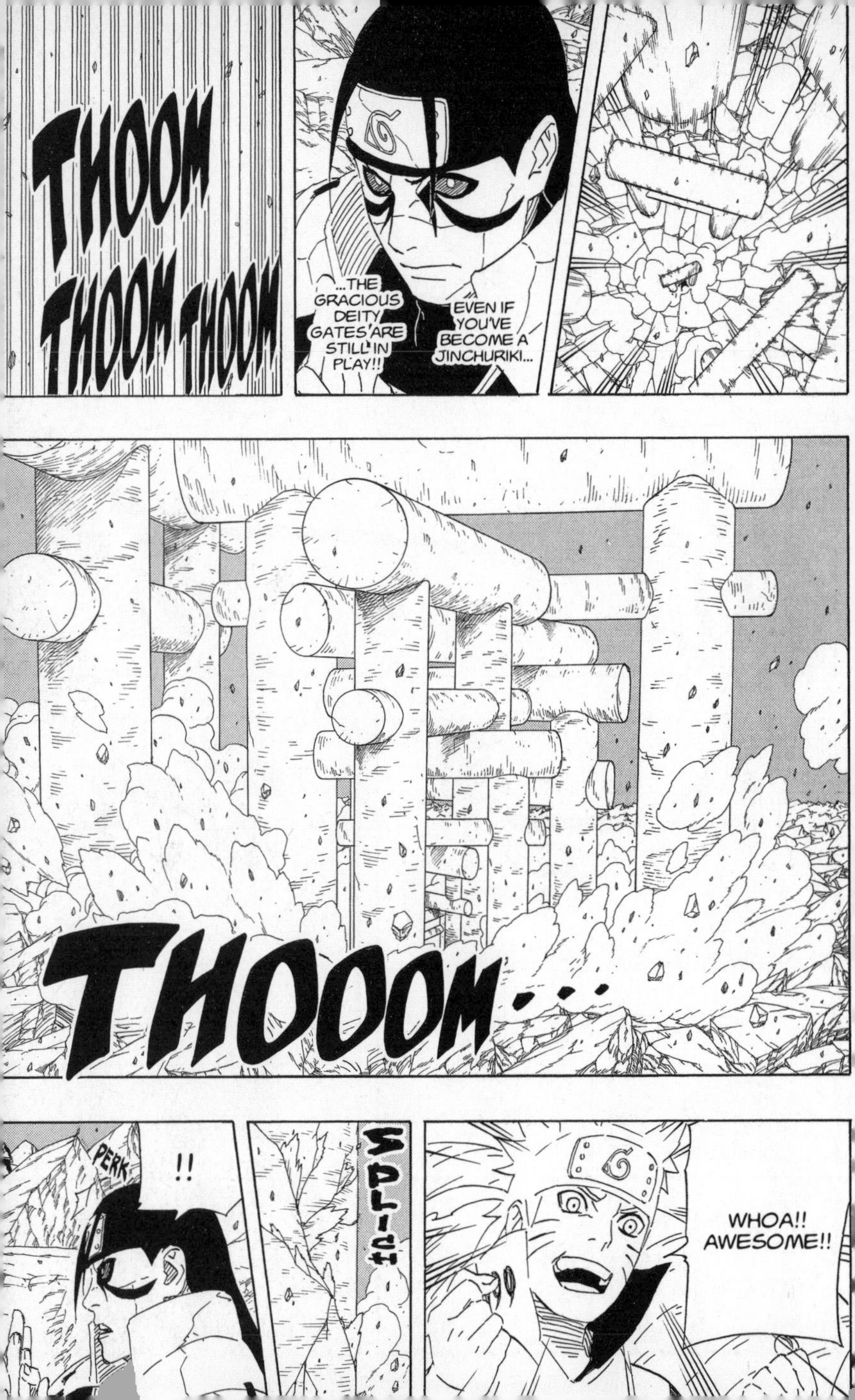

EVEN IF YOU'VE BECOME A JINCHURIKI...
...THE GRACIOUS DEITY GATES ARE STILL IN PLAY!!
THOOM
THOOM THOOM
THOOOM...
WHOA!! AWESOME!!
SPLICH
PERK
!!

KABOOOM

THK
G-G-

...

SUCH POWER...
THE SAGE ART: SEAL THAT HAD EVEN SUPPRESSED TEN TAILS...

FLICKER
FLICKER
FLICKER
ZOOOOM
ZW
GRD
GRGRD
GRD
GRGRD
!
!
!
!

FWMP
WHAP

IMPOS-SIBLE!

THE FOUR CRIMSON RAYS FORMATION !!

IS IT ME OR IS HE EVEN STRONGER THAN WHEN HE WAS GIGANTIC?

BEFORE, IT WAS JUST THROWING ITS POWER AROUND...

...BUT NOW IT'S APPARENTLY LEARNED TO FOCUS IT.

HE'S DESTROYED MY BARRIER!

WE DON'T KNOW WHAT THAT FELLOW WHO MADE TEN TAILS' POWER HIS OWN MIGHT DO!!

KEEP YOUR GUARD UP, ALL!!

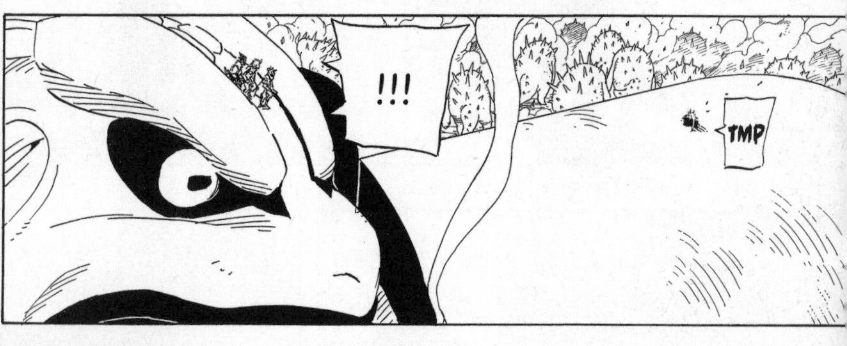

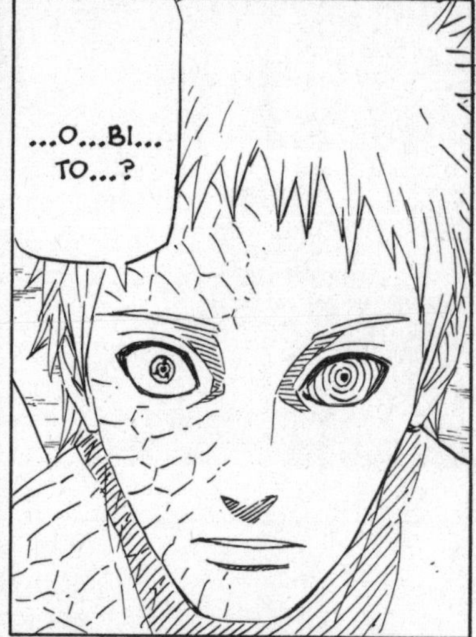

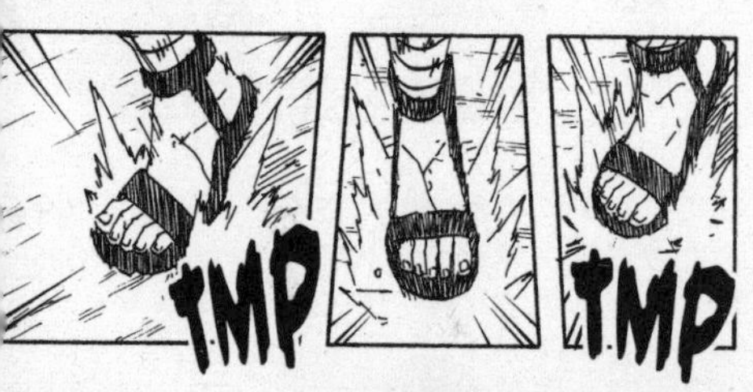

TO BE BLUNT, THIS GUY'S...

...STRONGER THAN ME!!

NO OFFENSE, BUT IT APPEARS SO.
EVEN IF YOU REABSORB YOUR REMAINING DOPPELGANGERS, YOU'RE NO MATCH, ELDER BROTHER!
I KNOW. HOWEVER...

FSH...
IT WOULD BE FUN TO WATCH THE HOKAGE BEG FOR MERCY, BUT...
...I CANNOT WAIT ANY LONGER.

OBITO IS NOW JUST LIKE THE SAGE OF SIX PATHS.
I CAN'T LET HIM TAKE THE LEAD BEFORE I USE MY TRUMP CARD...

HUH?

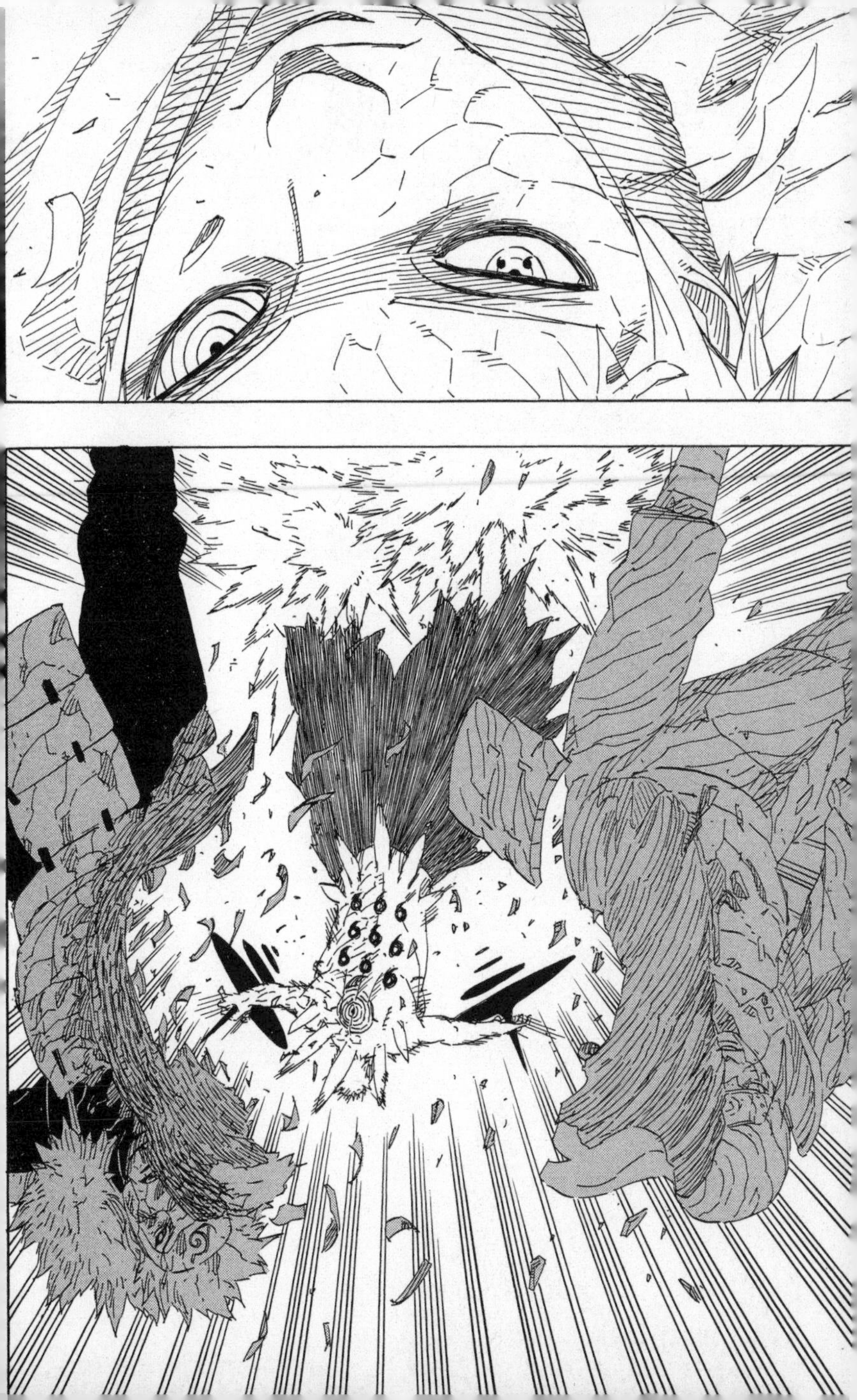

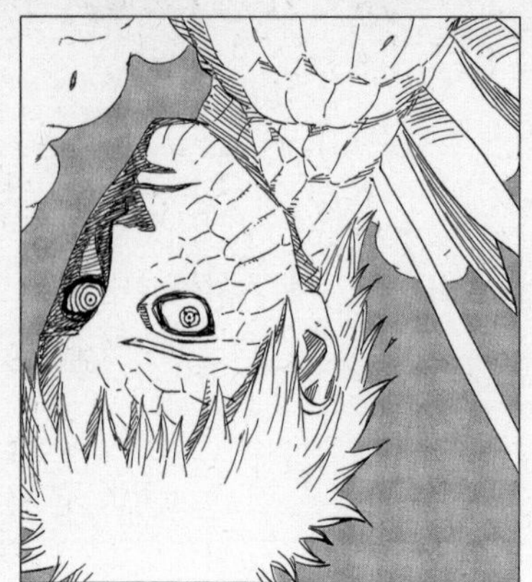

WHAT THE?!
SO SWIFT!
SARU! FOURTH! SCRAM!!
!
ROGER!
LORD SECOND'S ALREADY LAUNCHED HIS ATTACK PLAN!

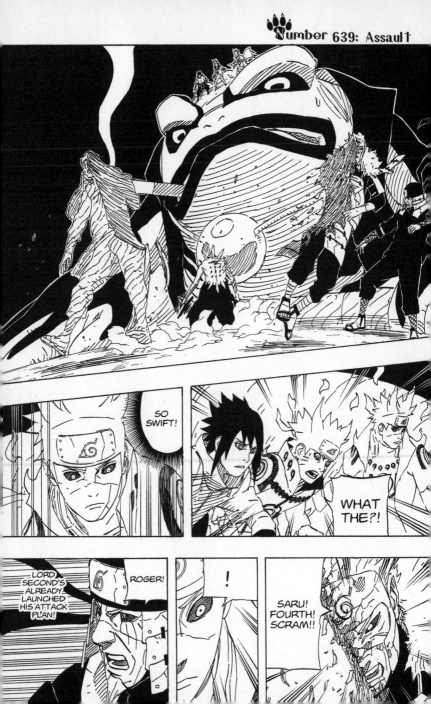

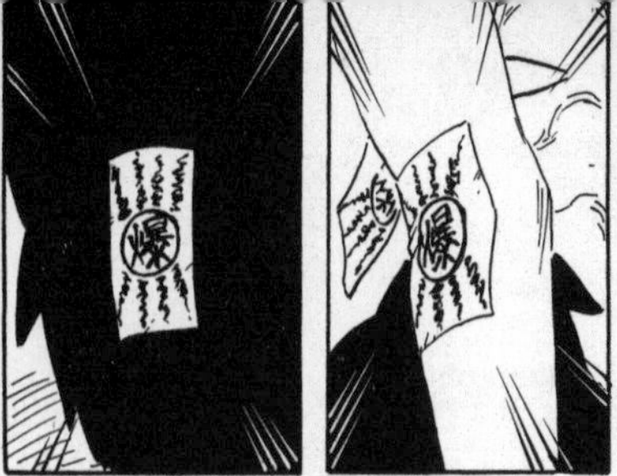

KRAKKRAKAK
KRAK
B'BOOF
LURCH

TAK
MINATO! GET YOURSELF AWAY!
LORD SECOND SURE WORKS QUICKLY!
FLYING RAIJIN JUTSU!
WOOSH
TMP
I CREATED THE EDOTENSEI JUTSU.
PLUS ANCILLARY JUTSU TO GO WITH IT...
THOUGH THIS IS THE FIRST TIME I'M USING IT ON MYSELF.
ZWUB
!
I SUS-PECTED THAT MIGHT NOT BE ENOUGH TO KILL YOU...
HERE IT COMES!
LORD SECOND'S SPECIAL...

TANDEM EXPLOSIVE TAGS!!
FLAP
THIS IS HOW IT'S DONE.
FLAP
EACH TAG SUMMONS YET MORE TAGS, RESULTING IN CONTINUOUS EXPLOSIONS.
FLASH
FOCALLY CONCENTRATED CONSECUTIVE EXPLOSIONS!
B-B-B-B-B-B-B-B-BOO
FSH

WHAT'S GOING ON? I CAN'T KEEP UP!
WHUMP
DON'T FRET! ALWAYS KEEP ONE EYE ON WHAT'S HAPPENING AROUND YOU!
!!

B-B-B-B-B-B-B-B-B-B-B-B-B-B-B-B-B-B-B-B-B-B-B-B-B-B-BOOM
TMP

I DON'T CARE IF THAT'S TEN TAILS' JINCHURIKI OR WHATEVER, BUT OUR LORDS HOKAGE ARE ENGAGED IN BATTLE!
WE MUST JOIN THEM!!
DON'T BE RASH! WE NEED TO--
ALL OF YOU!
YOU MUST NOT APPROACH HEEDLESSLY!!

...
HUFF
HUFF
HUFF

G-
G-
G-
□□□

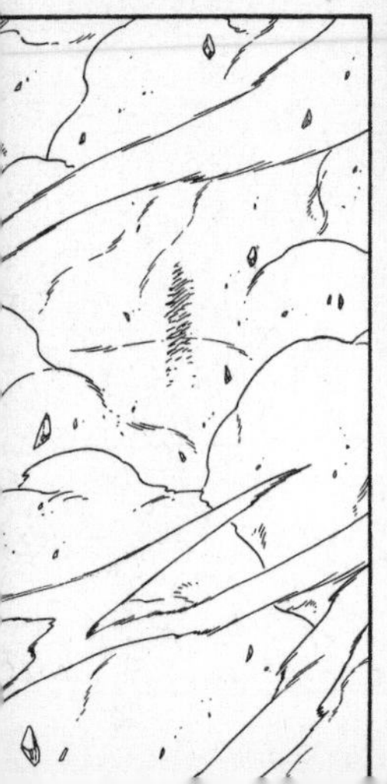

HE'S SOLID AS WELL AS SWIFT...
!
BOOF
PLUS HE HAS AN ATTACK THAT TURNS ALL TO DUST IN AN INSTANT!
...!
SHURIKEN SHADOW DOPPELGANGERS!!
FWOOOOOSH
SWOO

FSH
ZWW...
ZWOOSH
ZWP
ZWSH
IT'S SIMILAR TO OHNOKI'S PARTICLE STYLE, BUT ITS SHAPE IS FLUID...
IT CAN SHIFT TO BE EITHER OFFENSIVE OR DEFENSIVE, AND CAN BE CONTINUOUSLY MAINTAINED.

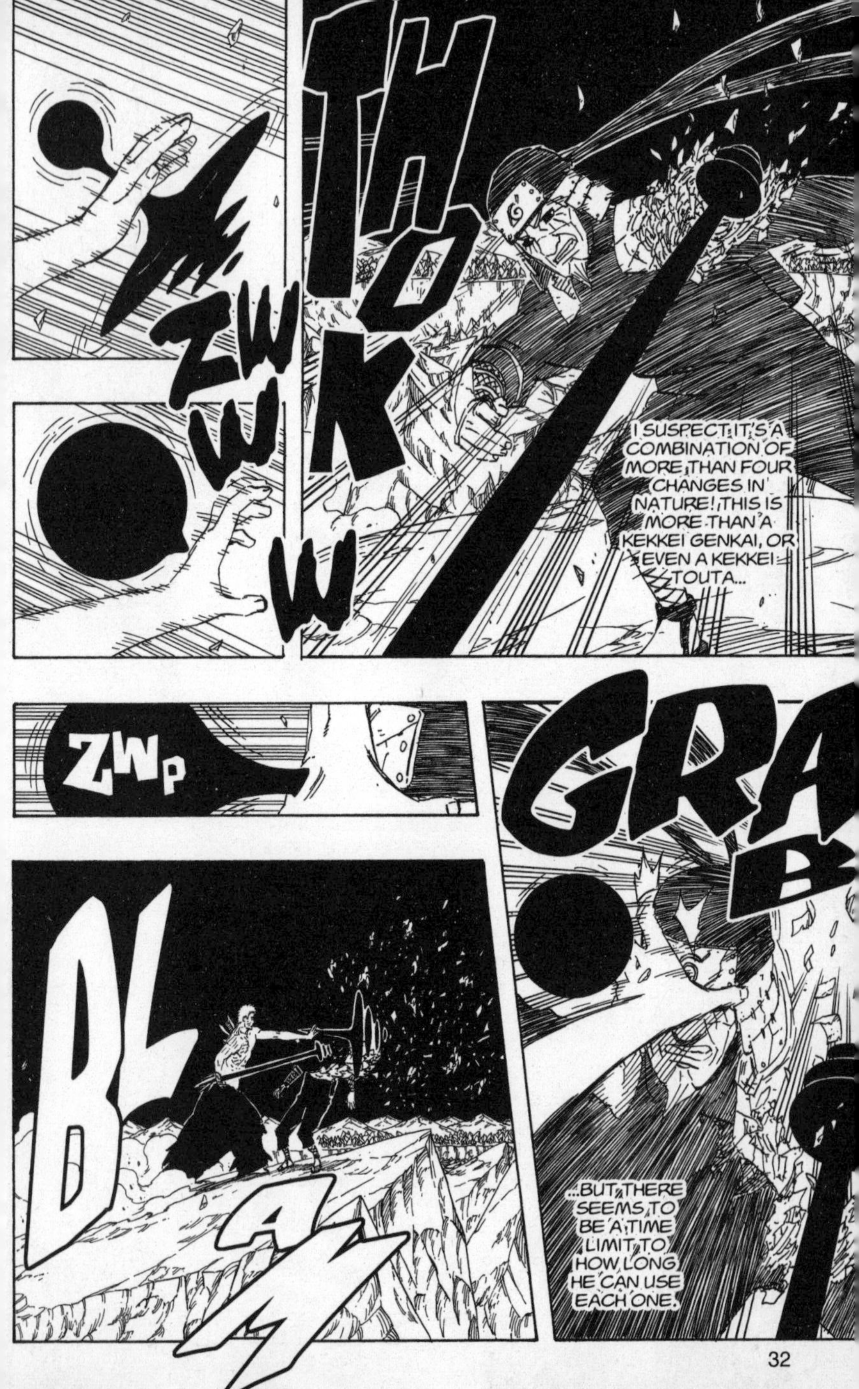
THOOM
I SUSPECT IT'S A COMBINATION OF MORE THAN FOUR CHANGES IN NATURE! THIS IS MORE THAN A KEKKEI GENKAI, OR EVEN A KEKKEI TOUTA...
ZWWWW
GRAB
ZWP
...BUT THERE SEEMS TO BE A TIME LIMIT TO HOW LONG HE CAN USE EACH ONE.
BLAM

PA!
YOU COULDN'T TELEPORT OLD MAN THIRD WITH YOUR JUTSU TOO?!
I CAN'T TELEPORT ANYTHING THAT I MYSELF, OR MY CHAKRA, ISN'T TOUCHING DIRECTLY.
QUIT YAPPING, NARUTO!
THE HOKAGE ARE ALL EDO-TENSEI.
THEY INTENTIONALLY ATTACKED HEAD-ON KNOWING THAT THEY WON'T DIE...
...IN ORDER TO CHECK OUT THE ENEMY'S MOVES AND ABILITIES.
STOP WORRYING AND ANALYZE THE BATTLE INSTEAD.
SO THAT'S SASUKE, HUH. HE'S BRIGHT.
THOUGH IT STILL TAKES A LITTLE WHILE FOR AN EDOTENSEI TO REGENERATE.
THUD

VWO
I'LL GO FIRST AND CREATE AN OPENING!
SHOOH

AT THIS POINT, I FEEL I NEED TO...
TAK

I'M DONE WAITING...
TMP
...HASHI-RAMA!

!

TMP
...
!!
BULGE BULGE BULGE
!

?
...?
...?

THIS IS OUR CHANCE TO TAKE IT DOWN!

TK

I'LL SUMMON MY ORIGINAL HERE, THEN...

I SEE... TEN TAILS HASN'T SYNCED COMPLETELY WITH ITS JINCHURIKI YET!

...IT'S TIME FOR MY RASEN-FLASH SUPER-CIRCLE DANCE HOWL STAGE THREE. IT'S BEEN A WHILE!
WSH
FSH
GAMAKICHI, BELOW!!
THK
UGH!!
WAH !!
!!

THOOM

HE PASSED UNDERGROUND ?!
TAK
JUST HIS UPPER BODY!!

!
SHOOM

SSH

!!

THAK
!
SWSH
!!
UGH!
WHAP WHAP
GAH!!

THMP

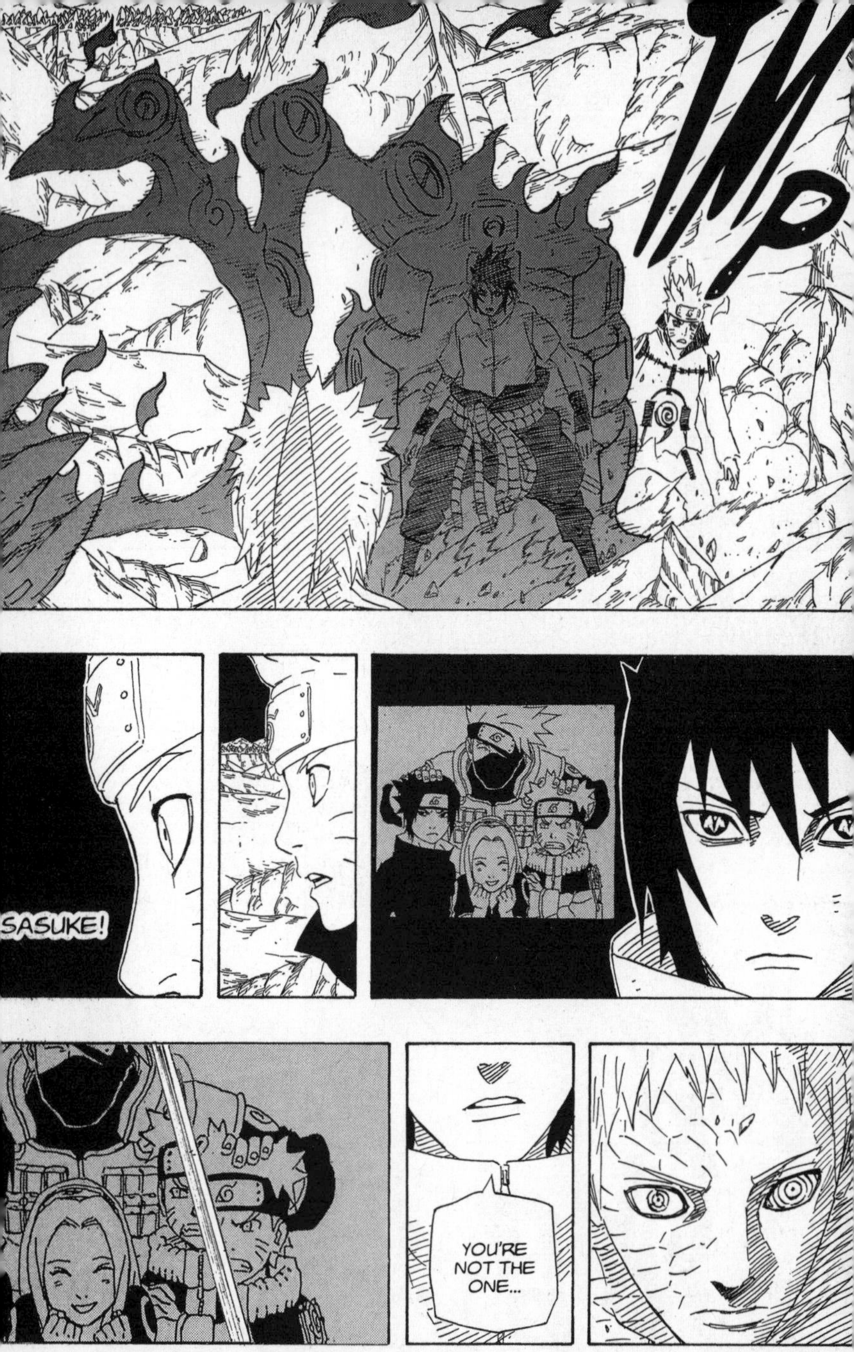

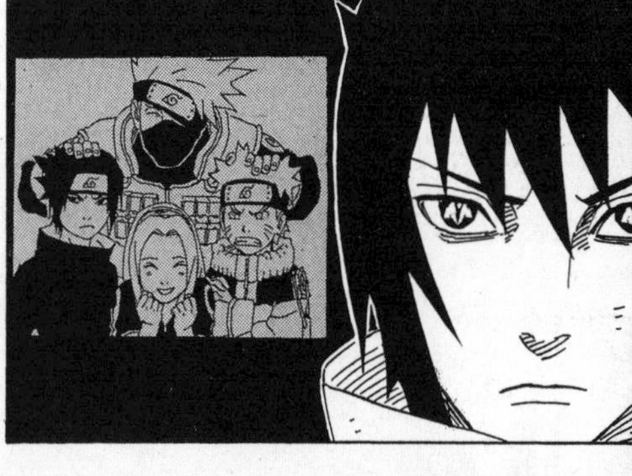

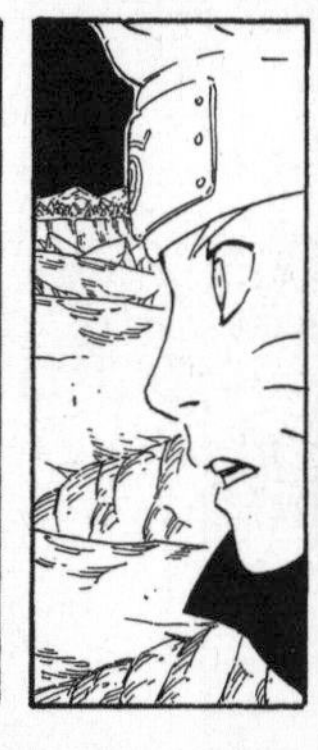

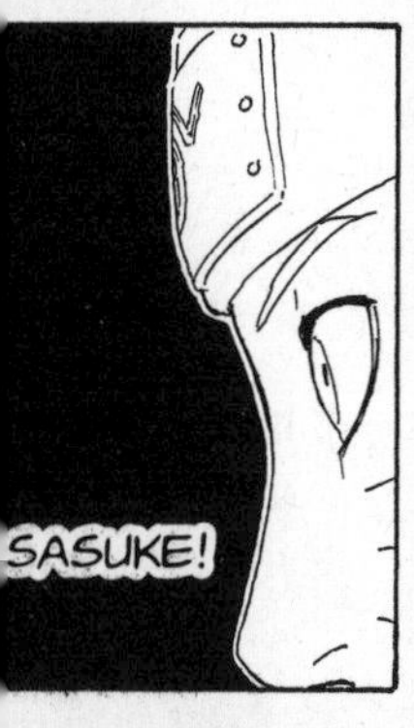
SASUKE!

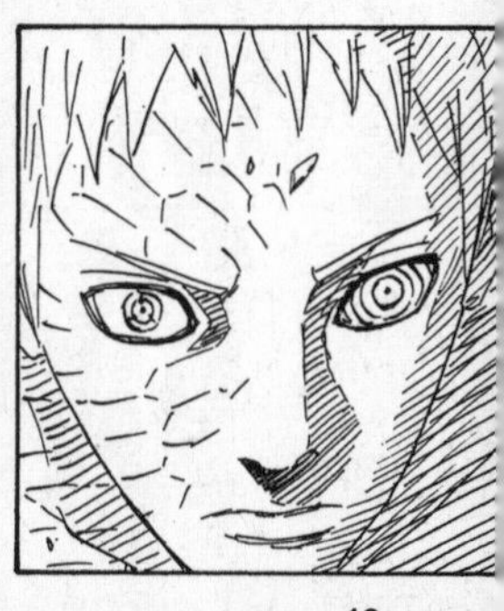

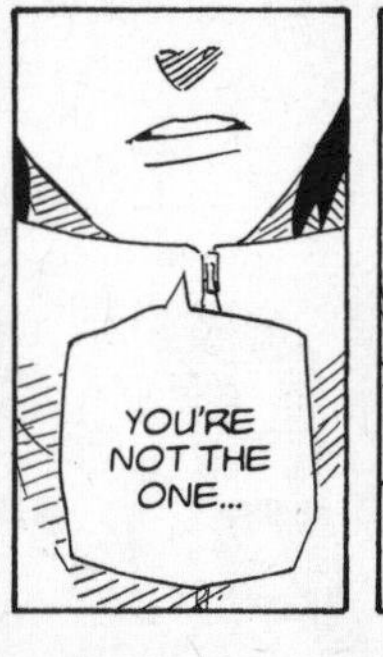
YOU'RE NOT THE ONE...

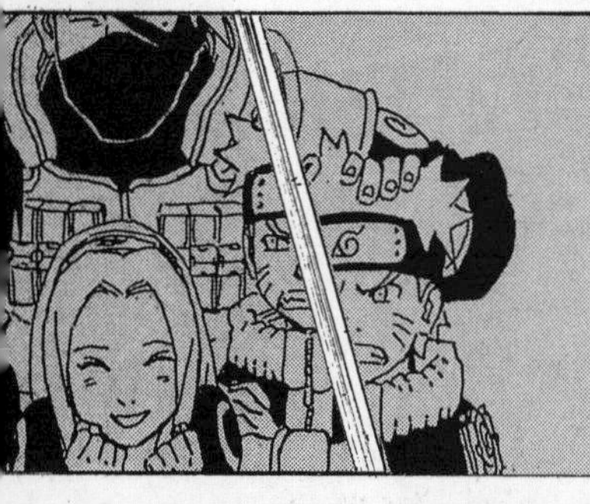

...WHO'S GOING TO SEVER THE PAST.
I AM!
!!
!!
GRAB
GRAB
BE IN TIME!!
FLYING RAIJIN JUTSU!!
SKID

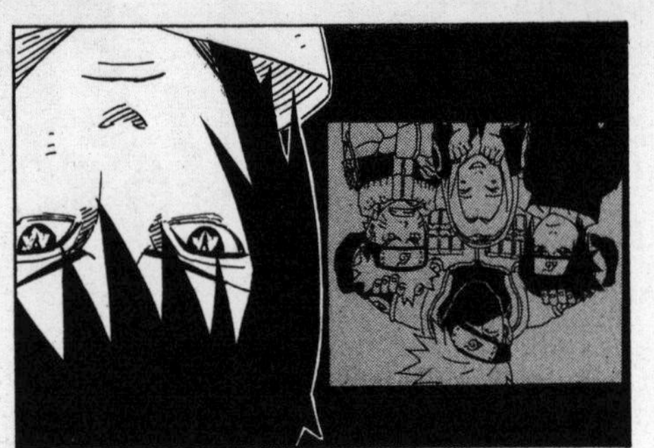

Number 640: Finally

SSH
SSH
WSH
WSH

...?
OWWW...
!
FFT
YIKES! I THOUGHT WE WERE GONNA DIE!!
"I CAN'T TELEPORT ANYTHING THAT I MYSELF, OR MY CHAKRA, ISN'T TOUCHING DIRECTLY."
!
...
LOOKS LIKE MY CHILD IS AS ACCOMPLISHED AS SASUKE.

HE'S LIKE A SNAKE!

ARRR... AAAAWR ...!
BULGE
BULGE
BULGE
SWOO
FSH
DNK
THOOM
BLAM
WHOOOOOOOOOOO...
?!!
FLASH

OOSH
WHOOOO
WOOOOOO

GGGGG

HE WENT AFTER YOUR DOPPEL-GANGER, PA?

?

WOOSH

WAFT
HE HIT HIMSELF WITH HIS OWN ATTACK.
HIS ATTACK MISSED!
IT LOOKS LIKE OBITO'S CONSCIOUSNESS IS MERELY CLINGING TO TEN TAILS' GREAT POWER...
HE BARELY HAS ANY CONTROL OVER IT!
GLAD HE MISSED CUZ THAT WILL KILL US.
WE CAN'T CARE-LESSLY APPROACH HIM.
THIS TIME, I'LL GET THE RASEN-FLASH SUPER-CIRCLE DANCE HOWL STAGE 3 IN FOR SURE!
SHUP
I'LL CREATE AN OPENING, YOU TWO IMMEDIATELY HIT HIM WITH YOUR STRONGEST COMBO!

THK THK THK

AND THEN...

...I WON'T HAVE ANY TIME FOR GIRLS!

RIGHT, MASTER?

GARGH!!

SNAP

RRIP...

SNAP
AHHHH!!!

RRIP...

HUFF
WEEZ

HERE I COME !!
OBITO!
WHO... ARE... YOU...?
...
GARGH !!
ZQUICH
RRIP
...!!
ZWW...
GLINT

AHHHHHHHHHHHH!

SNAP

SNAP

SNAP

SNAP

?!!
FINALLY...
...MASTER.
SHOOT!

...

PA!!

NARUTO, STAY FOCUSED!

!!

!

HE MAY HAVE GOTTEN ME, BUT I'M FINE!

FFT

I USED FLYING RAIJIN TO ESCAPE.

ARE YOU SURE?

!!

WHEN DID HE...?
AH!! HE ATTACHED IT TO ME SO IT WOULD TELEPORT ALONG WITH ME!
!!
FLASH

Number 641: You Two Are the Main Act!!

WH
!!
SH
FFT
YOU CAN HAVE THIS BACK.
!
PAT
WSH

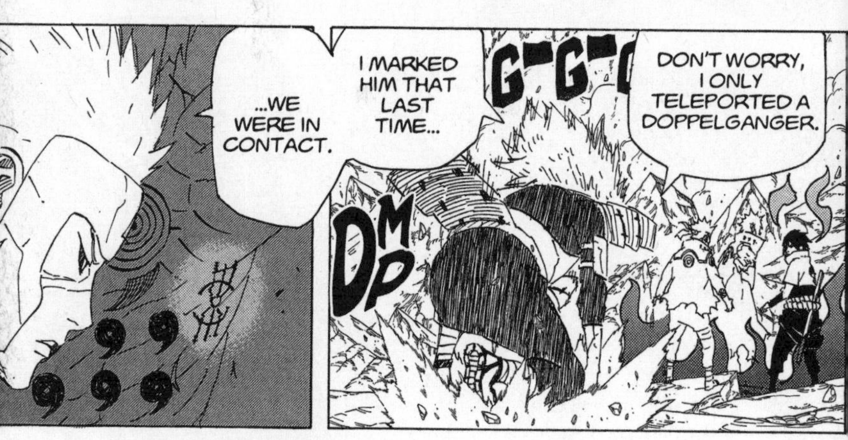

WOW!! YOU CAN COPY PA'S MOVE?!
VERY IMPRESSIVE, SECOND MOUNTAIN-SIDE IMAGE GUY!!
YOU KNOW, THE FOURTH IS USING ***MY*** MOVE.
PLUS, THAT'S ***LORD SECOND*** TO YOU!
CHOMP

GET OUT OF MY WAY, MADARA!!
TROMP
TROMP
TROMP
TROMP
TROMP

I DON'T HAVE MUCH TIME, BUT THERE'S SOMETHING I'VE GOT TO DO NOW!
ZOOOOSH

?
I'M TAKING ANOTHER CHUNK OF YOU!
THOOM
WH- WHOA!
IT'S LIKE THEY'RE ON A TOTALLY DIFFERENT LEVEL!
WAH!!
ARGH!!
THK DK
SO THIS IS THE BATTLE CAPACITY OF OUR PREDECES- SORS!
FOR SURE, WE'D JUST GET IN THEIR WAY IF WE TRIED TO JOIN IN.

EVEN A SMALL POWER CAN BE HELPFUL...

...DEPENDING ON HOW IT'S USED.
!
WE MAY NOT BE ANY HELP RIGHT NOW, BUT THERE MAY COME A TIME WHEN WE WILL BE NEEDED.

THAT YOU, SHIKA-MARU?
SO DON'T TAKE YOUR EYES OFF THE BATTLEFIELD...
...FOR IF SUCH A TIME ARRIVES...

...OUR POWER COULD CHANGE THE COURSE OF THIS WORLD!
AND THUS...

...WE CAN'T AFFORD TO RELAX AND LET OUR GUARDS DOWN FOR EVEN ONE SECOND!!

SHIKAMARU, YOU WOULD MAKE A GREAT HOKAGE.

THE ABILITY TO SWAY PEOPLE'S HEARTS...
...IS PRACTICALLY A REQUISITE OF ANY KAGE.
FWUMP
HE BLOCKED IT, HUH. HE'S FAST.
WE WON'T GET HIM BY JUST THROWING JUTSU IN HIS DIRECTION.

G'G
BO
OF
FWP
GLA
RE
BZT...
BZT...
IT SEEMS I'LL HAVE TO CREATE AN OPENING WITH MY...
...RASEN-FLASH SUPER-CIRCLE DANCE HOWL STAGE 3, AFTER ALL.
YOU'RE A BIT... OF AN ACCIDENTAL COMEDIAN.
I'D NORMALLY POKE FUN AT YOUR JUTSU NAMES...
...EXCEPT THAT THIS GUY WE'RE FACING'S ABSOLUTELY *NO JOKE.*

AMATERASU!!!

I SAID THAT I'D MAKE AN OPENING FOR YOU!
SASUKE! NARUTO !!

NO, WE WILL!
I'LL CREATE AN OPENING!
PA, Y'ALL CAN BE THE MAIN ACT!!
HARDLY A SURPRISE ATTACK.
I COULD TELL YOU WERE AMASSING CHAKRA IN YOUR LEFT EYE.

SWIRL
THWOK

!!
A DOPPEL-GANGER'S FLYING RAIJIN IS TOO SLOW.
THE TWO OF US WILL COMBINE OUR FLYING RAIJIN.
GO AHEAD AND PUT YOUR MARK ON ME TOO.
FSH
LET'S GO, FOURTH.
PAT
YEESH!
NARUTO, THIS TIME, ***I'LL MATCH YOUR CHAKRA LEVEL*** USING MY SHARINGAN.
SHEESH, NO NEED TO TURN IT INTO A COMPETITION!
YES, SIR. PLUS WITH THESE BODIES, WE CAN ALWAYS...
FSH

WIND STYLE, RASEN-SHURIKEN!!
INFERNO STYLE, FLAME CONTROL!!
THK
ZWP

!
A PINCER ATTACK?
FWD
?!!
?!

YOU TWO ARE THE MAIN ACT!!
?!
NOW!!
FLYING RAIJIN JUTSU!!!

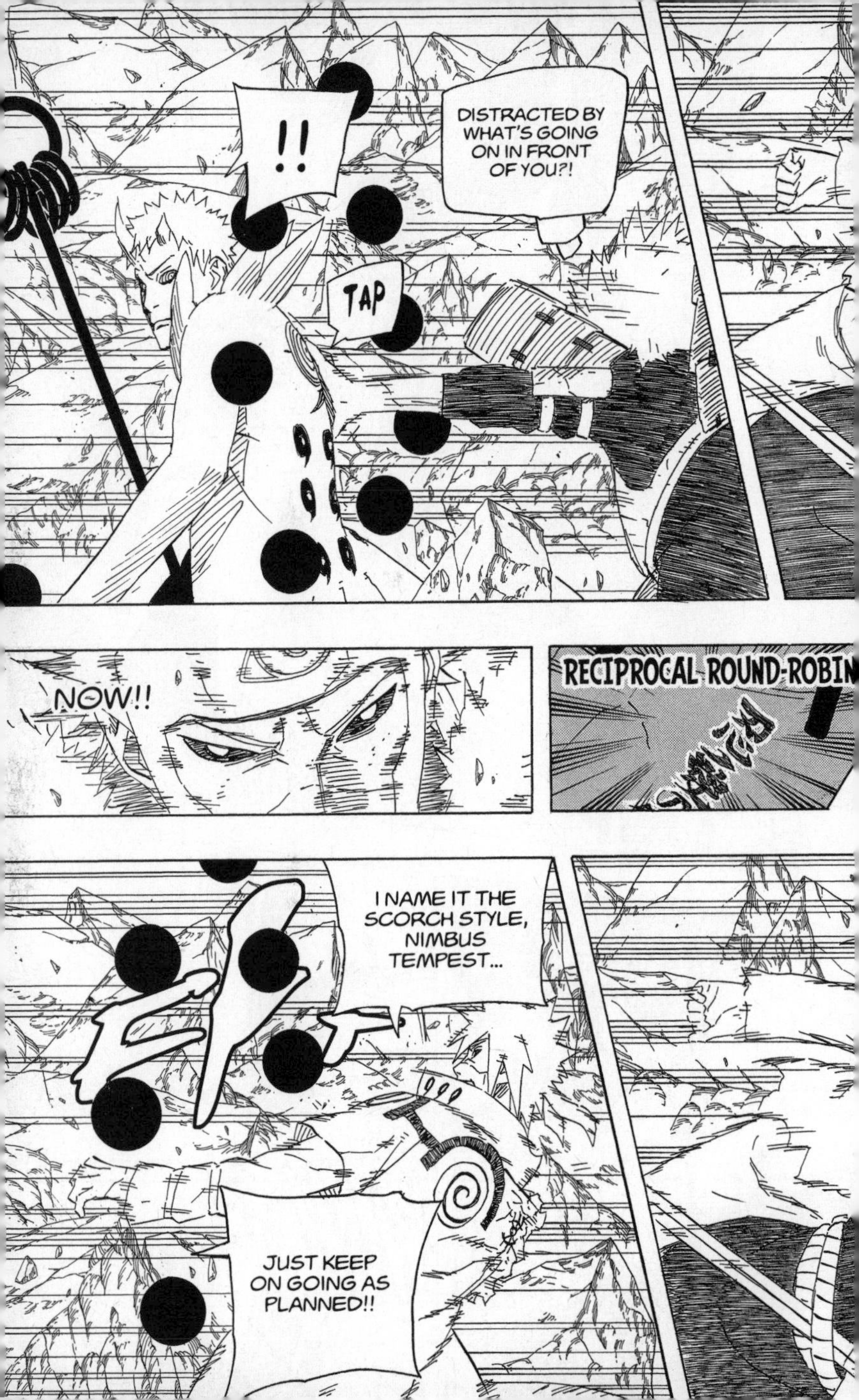
DISTRACTED BY WHAT'S GOING ON IN FRONT OF YOU?!
!!
TAP
RECIPROCAL ROUND-ROBIN
NOW!!
I NAME IT THE SCORCH STYLE, NIMBUS TEMPEST...
JUST KEEP ON GOING AS PLANNED!!

BLAM
TMP
THEY SWITCHED PLACES BY TELEPORT-ING!
VOOSH
!
WSH

YAH!!!
HINATA!
WHAT'S GOING ON WITH NARUTO AND SASUKE?
...
THE TWO OF THEM...
...ARE LAUGHING...
HUFF
HUFF
HUFF
HUFF

Number 642: An Opening

DIDJA GET HIM?!

HUFF

HUFF

ALL RIGHT!!

VWOOO
BZZSH
!
!

...
SWOO
NO EFFECT AT ALL...
WE HAVE TO AVOID THOSE BLACK TRANS-FORMING SPHERES, AND OUR ATTACKS DON'T WORK ON HIM...
HIS OFFENSE AND DEFENSE IS SO FAST...
WHAT A PAIN.
TAK
THIS GUY'S EVEN MORE PERFECT THAN HOW I IMAGINE MYSELF IN MY DREAMS!
IT'S LIKE HE'S TRULY OBTAINED DREAMLIKE POWER.
TMP
...
THAT'S ODD...
?!
YOU ONLY HAD AN ARM TORN OFF.
THERE SHOULD BE DUST SWIRLING AROUND TO RESTORE IT BY NOW.
...

I HAVE COME TO POSSESS THE SAME POWER AS THE ***FOUNDER OF SHINOBI.***
YOU CAN NO LONGER MEASURE ME BY THE STANDARDS YOU ARE USED TO.
...
DON'T TELL ME...
...YOUR JUTSU...
WHAT DOES HE MEAN?
FOURTH, TRY NOT TO GET SERIOUSLY WOUNDED ANY MORE.
EVEN THOUGH YOU'VE GOT AN EDOTENSEI BODY.
I SUSPECT THIS GUY IS USING JUTSU BASED ON SHADOW AND LIGHT STYLES THAT NULL ***ALL NINJUTSU!***
IN SHORT, EVEN WITH AN EDOTENSEI BODY, IF HE GETS YOU...

...YOU WON'T BE ABLE TO REGENERATE...
...AND CAN EVEN DIE!
...
ASSUME THAT RIGHT ARM OF YOURS IS PERMANENTLY GONE.
IN WHICH CASE, WE'LL NEED TO FIGHT HIM EVEN MORE CAREFULLY.
SHUP
SASUKE...
WHAT?
WE'RE GONNA HAVE TO TAKE THE LEAD. CAN YOU KEEP UP?
DON'T UNDER-ESTIMATE THE UCHIHA!
ALL RIGHT!!
I'LL UP MY KURAMA MODE AND UNDERGO FURTHER BIJU TRANS-FORMATION!!
BOOSH

FOOSH
?!

...
YOU'RE AS GOOFY AS YOUR FATHER, SO MUCH SO...
...THAT EVEN *HE'S* DUMB-FOUNDED.
...
S-SORRY.

...
...

HUH?
ARE YOU TRYING TO MAKE OUR SITUATION EVEN WORSE?

!!

!!

KURAMA, C'MON! LEND ME SOME MORE OF YOUR CHAKRA, WILL YA?!
YOU NEED TO DO WITHOUT NINE TAILS POWER FOR A BIT!
IF YOU WANT TO ENTER PERFECT BIJU MODE AS SOON AS POSSIBLE, YOU'LL HAVE TO FIGHT IN NORMAL MODE FOR A WHILE!
SYRUP GUN!!!
BULGE

SQUELCH
SPLAT

STRE...TCH
SQUELCH
...
...
HMM?
HOLD ON...
...
SNAP
OBITO, I THOUGHT WHAT YOU WANTED WAS TO BECOME HOKAGE?!
WHY ARE YOU DOING SUCH THINGS ?!
FSH
THIS IS MY CHANCE!!

A LECTURE NOW?
IT'S A LITTLE LATE FOR THAT... MASTER.
...
YOU'RE ALWAYS TOO LATE WHEN IT MATTERS MOST.
WHAT'S MASTER MINATO DOING?!
I'M ASKING YOU WHAT THE YELLOW FLASH IS UP TO!
I'M GLAD MY TEACHER WAS A HOKAGE.
...
IT MADE IT EASY TO GIVE UP ON BEING HOKAGE!

...

...

BUT WHY ATTACK KONOHA?
IN THE END, IT DOESN'T MATTER WHO YOU ARE...
四代目火影

YOU COULD SAY IT'S... FOR FUN, BUT ALSO AS PART OF A PLAN...
FOR THE SAKE OF WAR... BUT ALSO FOR THE SAKE OF PEACE.

IF I HAD ONLY REALIZED THAT THAT MAN WAS OBITO...
...I MAY HAVE BEEN ABLE TO STOP HIM!

I MIGHT NOT HAVE HAD TO MAKE NARUTO INTO NINE TAILS' JINCHURIKI!
SHOOF...
SNOO... SNOO...

...I MIGHT HAVE BEEN ABLE TO PREVENT KUSHINA FROM DYING!
AND THEN...

IF ONLY...

...I HAD NOTICED THAT THAT WAS OBITO!!

PERHAPS THE SHINOBI WORLD WOULDN'T HAVE ENDED UP LIKE THIS EITHER!!

YOU WERE MY TEACHER, AND YET YOU DIDN'T REALIZE IT WAS ME.
THAT'S JUST WHO YOU ARE, FUNDAMENTALLY.

HOW SAD...
YOU, WHO DIED A HERO HOKAGE, ARE BEING EXPOSED AS A DISGRACE IN FRONT OF YOUR SON.

THAT'S RIGHT.
A HOKAGE IS A PITIABLE EXISTENCE COMPARED TO WHAT I AM NOW.
ZWW

THE KID'S NOT A TOTAL GOOFBALL...
HE'S CAUGHT ON!

...
FSH
YOU, WHO COULDN'T BECOME HOKAGE, HAVE NO RIGHT TO INSULT ANY OF THEM!
NARUTO ...?
TAP
ESPECIALLY NOT MY PA WHO ACTUALLY BECAME HOKAGE!
...!
...!
WOSH

HOW DARE YOU PUT HIM DOWN !!!

GASH GASH
?!!
THAT WORKED ?!
...!
WHY? HOW?
IT'S EFFECTIVE! SO IT IS JUST AS I THOUGHT!
NINJUTSU MAY NOT WORK...

...BUT IT SEEMS SENJUTSU DOES!!
THAT SENJUTSU-USING MOUNT MYOBOKU TOAD'S ATTACK...
...WASN'T NULLIFIED OR ERASED.
STRE-TCH
SQUEL
WHRRRL
TAKE THAT, YOU BASTARD !!
BLAM

HE'S EVEN MASTERED THE SAME SENJUTSU AS MASTER JIRAIYA?!
!
HE'S GROWN INTO QUITE A SON, EH, MINATO?
IT'S NO WONDER HE MANAGED TO SWEET TALK MY OTHER HALF.

Number 643: Fist Bump

THAT'S WHY YOU SEALED MY LEFTOVER HALF INSIDE HIM...

...AS IF YOU WERE CONFIDENT THEY'D BE ABLE TO WORK TOGETHER.

...WHAT THIS WORLD HAS BECOME, RIGHT NOW.
HE'S NOT THAT NEWBORN BABE ANY-MORE.
NARUTO, LISTEN UP. I'VE GOT SOMETHING TO TELL YOU.
IN FACT, TOMORROW IS...
!!

...
GGGG
SWOOOO
!
IT'S JUST LIKE I THOUGHT!
I CAN'T BELIEVE TEN TAILS' JINCHURIKI HAS SUCH A WEAKNESS.
SKOP
SZZZZZ...
AND WITH TEN TAILS INSIDE ME, I CAN'T PASS THROUGH THINGS EITHER.
WHAT A BOTHER...

TMP
SAGE MOVES WILL WORK!!
SAGE POWER?

TOAD ATTACKS ARE SENJUTSU— THEY USE NATURE ENERGY.
COME TO THINK OF IT, WHEN I TRIED TO GAUGE TEN TAILS' POWER, IT WAS NATURE ENERGY ITSELF.
SO MAYBE YOU CAN COUNTER NATURE ENERGY WITH NATURE ENERGY...
NOT THAT I REALLY UNDERSTAND IT.

I'M JUST GLAD I LEARNED SENJUTSU!!
ALL RIGHT! NEXT UP, HE'S GETTING A FROG PUNCH TO THE FACE!
WHAP

WAFT

HE INSTANTLY GRASPED HOW TO USE THE FLYING RAIJIN WITH ME...
...AND HAS EVEN MASTERED SAGE POWER.
FSH

I FEEL LIKE I'M FIGHTING ALONGSIDE ELDER -BROTHER!

...

...

BOOF

IT CLEARLY WORKED, BUT HE'S RECOVERED ALREADY, AND NOW HE'S GUARDING HIS BACK.
IF WE TELEPORT BEHIND HIM CARELESSLY, WE MIGHT GET ERASED.

I OUGHT TO START PREPARING FOR THE TSUKUYOMI. LET'S TIDY UP...
FSH

THDTHD

G G G
!
!
!
...!
THERE IS NOTHING...
...WORTH SAVING IN THIS REALITY.

...!

THIS WORLD IS ALREADY DEAD.
WAFT...

GWEEEEN

!!

!!

...
HEY, THIS IS SUPER BAD!
FOUR OF THEM? ALL AT ONCE?!

EVEN IF WE ALL WERE TO CREATE AN EARTH WALL, IT WOULD NOT BE ENOUGH!
THERE'S TOO MANY OF 'EM!

WHAT TO DO?! THINK, MAN!

G-G-
KEEP FIGHTING!!
THOOM

DO NOT GIVE UP, ALL! I AM WITH YOU!!
WE ONLY NEED TO CHANGE THE SPHERES' TRAJECTORIES !!
THE OTHER HOKAGE WILL ALSO TAKE MEASURES AND REPEL THEM ACROSS THE OCEAN!!
I ASK THAT YOU ALL WORK ON ERECTING AN EARTH-STYLE WALL!
I'LL USE THE DEEP FOREST EMERGENCE TO LAUNCH AND GUIDE THEM TOWARD THE OCEAN!
BOOF
I WON'T LET YOU!
FSH
ZWP

?!!
THK
THK
THK
VOOSH
VOOSH
VOOSH

THK
THK
THK
SIX CRIMSON RAY FORMATION!!
WOOSH
WOOSH
WOOSH

A BARRIER !!
H-HEY...
DON'T TELL ME WE'RE...

HE'S TRAPPED EVERYONE INSIDE THE BARRIER, PLUS MADE IT SO WE CAN'T EXPEL THE BIJU BOMBS!

ZZMMMMMPPP
ENDGAME.

OUR ONLY CHANCE NOW IS TO TELEPORT THOSE SPHERES OUTSIDE THE BARRIER USING THE FLYING RAIJIN.
FOURTH, CAN YOU HANDLE TWO OF THEM?!

SINCE WE CAN'T MARK THEM, I CAN ONLY TAKE ON ONE.

BUT THERE IS ONE WAY...
WE COULD...

YOU INTEND TO TELEPORT THE STALK ITSELF OUTSIDE?
YOU THINK I'D LET YOU DO THAT?
YOU CANNOT SAVE ANYONE!

...

!
SHUP
PA, I DON'T KNOW IF IT'LL WORK OR NOT, BUT I'VE GOT AN IDEA.

BUMP FISTS WITH ME?
FSH

...?

...

BUMP

YO, MY OTHER HALF, HOW YA BEEN?
WOULDJA MIND SHARING SOME OF YOUR CHAKRA WITH ME?
?!
TO BE ASKED A FAVOR FROM MYSELF IS A BIT WEIRD...
NARUTO, MINATO'S USELESS. HE CAN'T DO ANYTHING.
HE COULDN'T EVEN PROTECT YOUR MOTHER!
...
NOR HIS OWN SUBORDINATES.
...
YOU KNOW WHAT TOMORROW IS, DON'T YOU?

...
IT'S THE ANNIVERSARY OF MINATO AND KUSHINA'S DEATH.
THE DAY BOTH OF YOUR PARENTS DIED.
IN *THIS* WORLD, IT'S *OVER* WHEN YOU DIE.
WAFT
WAFT
YOU SEE...
OH, RIGHT, WHICH MEANS...
...IT'S ALSO THE DAY *I WAS BORN!*
!
...
SO YOU SEE, IT'S NOT OVER...
...
ZWW...

...CUZ I EXIST IN THIS WORLD!!!
BWOOF
LET'S DO IT, PA!!!

...
OUR NARUTO SURE HAS GROWN REAL STRONG...
...KUSHINA!
YEAH !!

BUMP

Number 644: I Know

THANK GOODNESS FOR THE CHAKRA OF YOU TWO! IT'S JUST AS I THOUGHT.
YEAH... WE TWO USED TO BE ONE AFTER ALL.
PLUS...
...THOSE TWO ARE PARENT AND CHILD.

...

G-
G-G-
HE'S PLANNING TO TRAP US INSIDE THIS BARRIER AND BLOW US UP ALONG WITH IT!!
WHAT CAN WE DO?!!
BLAM
THE HOKAGE'S BARRIER DIDN'T LET BIJU BOMBS THROUGH EITHER.
AS FAR AS I CAN TELL, THE BARRIER LOOKS RED.
I THINK IT'S ACCURATE TO SAY THAT THIS ONE'S LIKELY TO BE ON PAR WITH THE HOKAGE'S!
BWF
WITH OUR LEVEL OF STRENGTH, IT'S IMPOSSIBLE FOR US TO SMASH THROUGH IT, IN WHICH CASE...
BOOM
GLP GLP
...
GAH!! NOTHING'S COMING TO MIND, PA!!

WHAT'S YOUR PLAN, NARUTO?

JUST...

...GIVE ME SOME TIME TO FOCUS...

...

I'M SO SORRY...

NARUTO...

I'M SURE IT'S BEEN A LONG, HARD ROAD FOR YOU UP UNTIL NOW!

THE REAL TOUGH PART IS ABOUT TO START NOW, PA!

PLIP
?!!
!!
BLIP
PLIP

ZWOOOSH
!!
TH-THIS IS NARUTO'S!
PLIP
PLIP

IT HADN'T GONE OUT?!
I NOTICED IT WHEN I HEALED EVERYONE.
IT SEEMS IT HAD MERELY SHRUNK DOWN.

IT'S ACTUALLY BIGGER AND STRONGER THAN BEFORE!!
ZWWW...

HAVE YA NOTICED, EIGHT-O? ♪
I SENSE TWO NINE TAILS, ONE LIGHT AND ONE DARK, YO!
THIS ISN'T JUST NINE TAILS...

YOU'RE THINKING ABOUT PROTECTING US FROM THAT ATTACK WITH THIS CHAKRA, NARUTO?!
JUGO.
!!
SASUKE, THIS IS LOOKING BAD. LET'S ESCAPE TO OUTSIDE THIS BARRIER!
USE THE SNAKE REVERSE-SUMMONING.
TMP
THAT WAS ALREADY MY PLAN.
I'LL TAKE YOU AND NARUTO WITH ME.
I HAVEN'T GIVEN YOU TWO ANY OF MY CHAKRA YET!
GET OVER HERE, WILL YA?!
HMPH... WHAT'S YOUR CHAKRA GONNA ACCOMPLISH?
THERE'S NO TIME! JUST DO IT!!

I CAN'T BELIEVE HE SHARED HIS CHAKRA WITH EVERY OTHER SHINOBI!
HE'S GOT ALMOST AS MUCH CHAKRA AS I!

!
NO! ACTUALLY, THIS HAS NINE TAILS' CHAKRA MIXED IN...

THAT WON'T HELP YOU WITHSTAND THE SHOCK WAVE OF FOUR TEN TAIL'S BIJU BOMBS EXPLODING TOGETHER.

BEGONE!
FSH

BL
!
!
VOOSH

BWWF

GG-GG
FIZZZZZ ZZZZ
PEEL
FIZZZZ
G-G-G-G
G-G-G-G-G-G
WHAT THE...?

?!
WHAT HAPPENED?
...**OUTSIDE** THE BARRIER!
IT WAS AN ART OF TELEPORTATION.
NARUTO'S MANAGED TO MASTER **THAT** TOO?!
THIS ISN'T JUST NARUTO'S CHAKRA...

THIS CHAKRA PROTECTED US AGAIN!!
NOT QUITE... CHECK IT OUT.
CHOJI, LOOK OVER THERE! WE'RE...

HE MOVED EVERYONE USING THE FOURTH HOKAGE'S FLYING RAIJIN JUTSU!

FOURTH...
NOW YOU'VE SAVED ALL OF SHINOBI-KIND FOR A **SECOND** TIME.

I'VE STILL FAILED MORE TIMES THAN THAT, SO...
HUF
HUF
...I MUST CON- TINUE MAKING AMENDS.

...

WHAT DID YOU DO?
!

PA JUST TELEPORTED EVERYONE OUTSIDE THE BARRIER.
EVERYONE, WITH ***THAT*** JUTSU?

I CAN'T TELEPORT ANYTHING THAT I MYSELF, OR MY CHAKRA, ISN'T TOUCHING, EVEN INDIRECTLY.
BUT HOW?

CUZ...
...I'D SHARED KURAMA'S CHAKRA WITH EVERYONE EARLIER!

SO IF PA AND OUR CHAKRA AND EVERYBODY WERE TO UH, ER...
...IN-DIRECT-LY...
RIGHT! IF WE ARE ALL IN INDIRECT CONTACT WITH EACH OTHER, IT'D WORK!

SO I CONNECTED PA'S CHAKRA WITH MINE AND KURAMA'S! THAT'S ALL!

HE'S USING THE PRINCIPLE OF SHADOW DOPPEL-GANGERS.
EVEN IF YOU SPLIT UP AND DISPERSE YOUR CHAKRA...
...AS LONG AS YOU KEEP EVEN A LITTLE BIT THERE WITHOUT PUTTING IT OUT...
ORIGINAL BODY

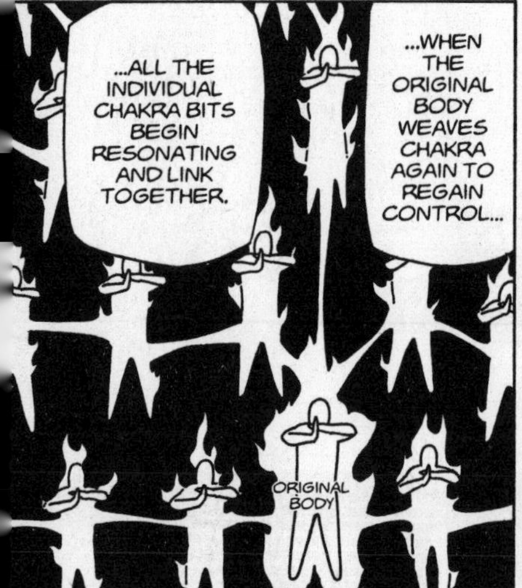
...WHEN THE ORIGINAL BODY WEAVES CHAKRA AGAIN TO REGAIN CONTROL...
...ALL THE INDIVIDUAL CHAKRA BITS BEGIN RESONATING AND LINK TOGETHER.
ORIGINAL BODY

IN SHORT, BY JOINING HIS CHAKRA TO THE FOURTH'S...
NA-RUTO
FOURTH
...NARUTO LINKED FOURTH TO THE REST OF HIS CHAKRA RESIDING IN EVERYONE ELSE.

RIGHT, NARUTO?
HUH?! DID I?
NEVER MIND...

OLD MAN SECOND, YOU SURE KNOW A LOT ABOUT MY SHADOW DOPPEL-GANGERS TOO!
I CAME UP WITH THAT JUTSU!
IT'S MY JUTSU!

...

YEAH, LET'S TRY IT.
THERE'S NOTHING WE CAN'T DO IF WE BORROW NINE TAILS'... I MEAN, KURAMA'S POWER.
ALL RIGHT! THEN LET'S ALL FOUR OF US JOIN FORCES!!
...ALL FOUR OF US, EH...
YOU TREAT US LIKE WE'RE HUMAN TOO... WHAT KIND OF CHILDREARING HAS LED TO THIS, EH? HEH HEH HEH.
...
NARUTO...
HUH?!
GUYS DON'T NEED TO TALK!
I KNOW ALREADY!
I WISH THERE WAS MORE TIME TO TALK TO THE GROWN-UP YOU...
I'VE...
...MET MA'S CHAKRA...
...!
SO MUCH! THERE'S SO... SO... MUCH...!
THERE REALLY IS... SO MUCH MORE I WANT... TO TELL YOU...
I WANT TO BE WITH YOU LONGER... I LOVE YOU.

...
...I'M SORRY, MINATO... I TALKED TOO MUCH...
NO, NO... IT'S ALL RIGHT...
NARUTO...
MY WORDS TO YOU AS YOUR FATHER...
WHAT YOU WANNA SAY...
...IS DITTO GABBY, CHATTERBOX MA, RIGHT?!
SEE, I KNOW ALREADY!

VSH VSH
IT'S QUITE FAMILIAR.
THIS FEELING...
Number 645: Two Powers
WE'RE TOTALLY BEING DRIVEN INTO A CORNER...
THAT'S RIGHT! IT'S JUST LIKE WHEN I WAS...
...WITH KUSHINA.
...AND YET, I STILL FEEL THAT WE CAN DO ANYTHING.
SWOO...

I FEEL POWER WELLING UP INSIDE ME!
LET'S GO!!
ZW
TAK
SH
!!
!
NARUTO'S GOT THIS MUCH CHAKRA...?
NARUTO, LETTING LOOSE A VIGOROUS SHOUT AND SHOWING OFF IS ALL WELL AND GOOD...
...BUT DON'T TELL ME YOU'VE ALREADY FORGOTTEN THAT **NOTHING OTHER THAN SENJUTSU** WORKS AGAINST HIM?
I KNOW YOU'RE NOT AN IDIOT...
DMP
...

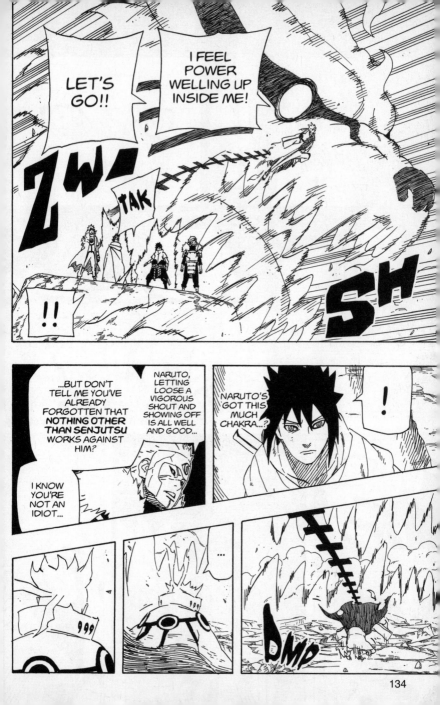

THAT'S RIGHT!!!
OKAY, YOU'RE AN EVEN BIGGER FOOL THAN MY ELDER BROTHER!
ALL THAT CHAKRA AND IT'S BEING WASTED ON HIM...
OR PERHAPS NOT QUITE THE SAME FEELING?
GWA HA HA HA! YOU'VE ALREADY SURPASSED ALL PREVIOUS HOKAGE...
GUFFAW GUFFAW
...IN STUPIDITY!
SHADDUP!! STUPID, STUPID KURAMA!
GWA HA HA HA! FOOLS ARE EASILY LIKED AND TRUSTED BY OTHERS!
BUT DON'T YOU MIND! THERE'S NO NEED TO WORRY...
HMPH
I-I NEVER REALLY CARED ABOUT BEING STUPID, Y'KNOW!!
NO, NO, NOT THAT...

I MEANT THAT YOU MIGHT BE ABLE TO UNDERGO SAGE TRANSFORMATION...
...WHILE IN BIJU STATE!
HUH?!

LISTEN, YOU MAY HAVE FORGOTTEN, BUT...
...IT HAPPENED WHEN YOU FACED OFF AGAINST PAIN NAGATO.
I GOT SO IRKED BY WHAT HE WAS SAYING, THAT...
...MY CHAKRA LEAKED OUT, EVEN THOUGH YOU WERE IN SAGE MODE AT THE TIME.

MY POWER AND YOUR SAGE POWER ACTUALLY SYNCED TOGETHER.

MMM...
FOR REAL?
...

OH!!
YOU SAY THAT, BUT BACK WHEN I WAS UNDERGOING SAGE TRAINING...
BRRR
...YOU INTERFERED WITH GRAMPS SAGE'S SAGE JUTSU, REMEMBER?!!
SH
?!
ARGH!
THWUMP
WAP
THAT'S BECAUSE I HAD NO INTEREST IN SHARING SPACE WITH TOADS!
PLUS, IT STUCK IN MY CRAW THAT YOU WOULD RELY ON SENJUTSU WHEN YOU HAD MY CHAKRA!!
!
YOU STUBBORN BASTARD...
THAT WOULD BE YOU!!
SNEER
WAGGLE
SO WHAT I'M TRYING TO SAY...
...IS THAT I'M WILLING TO LET YOU USE BOTH MY POWER AND SAGE POWER RIGHT NOW!!
WHAT'S STUBBORN ABOUT THAT, EH?!!
YOU JUST CAN'T BE UP FRONT ABOUT YOUR FEELINGS, CAN YOU...?
SNEER
YOU BASTARD! GIVE ME THE RESPECT I DESERVE!
LOOM

HAH, YOUR FAULT FOR LIKING AND TRUSTING ME.
FEH!
NOW THEN!
FSH

YOU'VE GOT THE SAME ME INSIDE YOU AS YOUR SON.
YOU OUGHT TO BE ABLE TO PROVIDE POWERFUL SUPPORT TO HIM.
...
YEAH.

ZWOOSH
I KNOW THAT ALREADY!
TAK

GLINT

TMP

...

?!

I'M ABSORBING NATURE ENERGY A LOT FASTER IN THIS STATE!
SHOOO...

I'LL HAVE SOME JUTSU PREPARED TOO!

ALL RIGHT THEN!!

NARUTO, ADD SENJUTSU TO THE RASENGAN!!
GOTCHA!!
OLD MAN SECOND!!

TAP
LET'S DO IT!
TAP
JUST FORGE AHEAD... WE'LL WARD OFF HIS ATTACKS WITH OUR CHAKRA!!
...!
BOOF

THOK
WHAP

THOK
RASENGAN!!!

BAM
BOOM

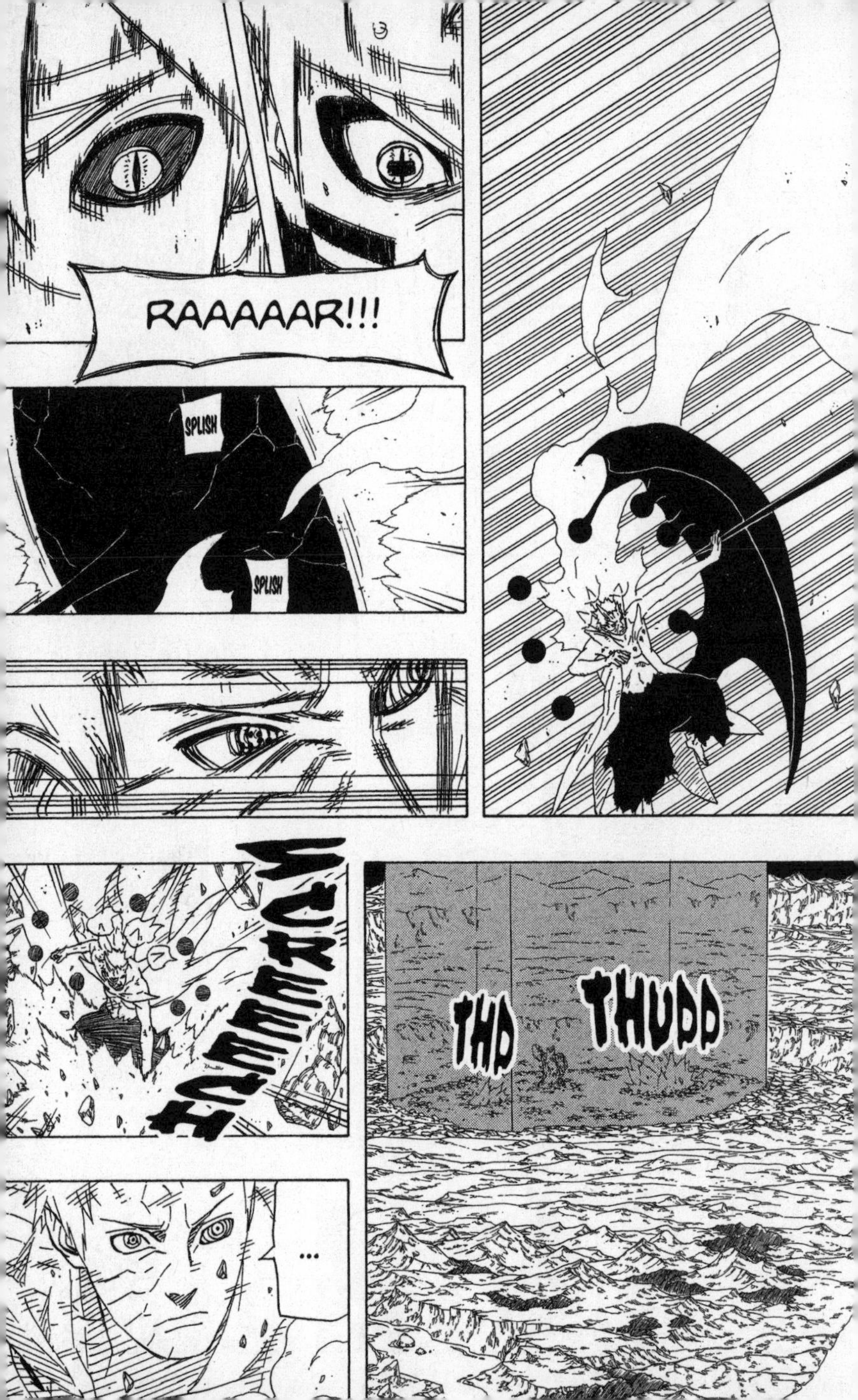
RAAAAAR!!!
SPLISH
SPLISH
THD
THUDD
SCREEEECH
...

KLATTER
KLATTER
THAT BLACK THING SURE IS SOLID, DARN IT!!
HE USED IT DEFENSIVELY THIS TIME.
HE SAW IT COMING, UNSURPRISINGLY.
PLOP
PLOP
USING ONLY THE FLYING RAIJIN ISN'T ENOUGH...
WE JUST NEED TO WRECK THAT BLACK THING, THAT'S ALL!
BUT HOW?
...LET'S TRY ADDING SENJUTSU TO A BIJU BOMB!
ZWWW
'KAY!
THIS TIME...
NICE! GOOD THINKING!
YOU MIGHT JUST BECOME A GREATER HOKAGE THAN ELDER BROTHER!
HEY, OTHER KURAMA, YOU HELP TOO!
OF COURSE!
IT IS...

...A FAMILIAR FEELING, AFTER ALL!

ZWW
SWOO...
...
WITH PERFECT CONTROL OVER THIS MUCH CHAKRA?
THIS IS NARUTO NOW?
HOW FAR...
...WILL YOU...
CLENCH
NO HARM IN TAKING MEASURES EARLY.
KL
AP

ZWOOO
LET'S START THIS!
ZWOOO
?!
LURCH
LURCH
LURCH
!

!
HE'S LAUNCHING THE INFINITE TSUKUYOMI ALREADY?!
THOOM
BULGE BULGE
TH-THOOM

ZW
WWWWWWW...
ZQUILCH...
KRK
KRK
KRK
FWMP FWMP FWMP
I'LL SUSPEND THE BARRIER FOR NOW...
VWOOOSH
ZWW
ZWOOOOO

Number 646: Divine Tree

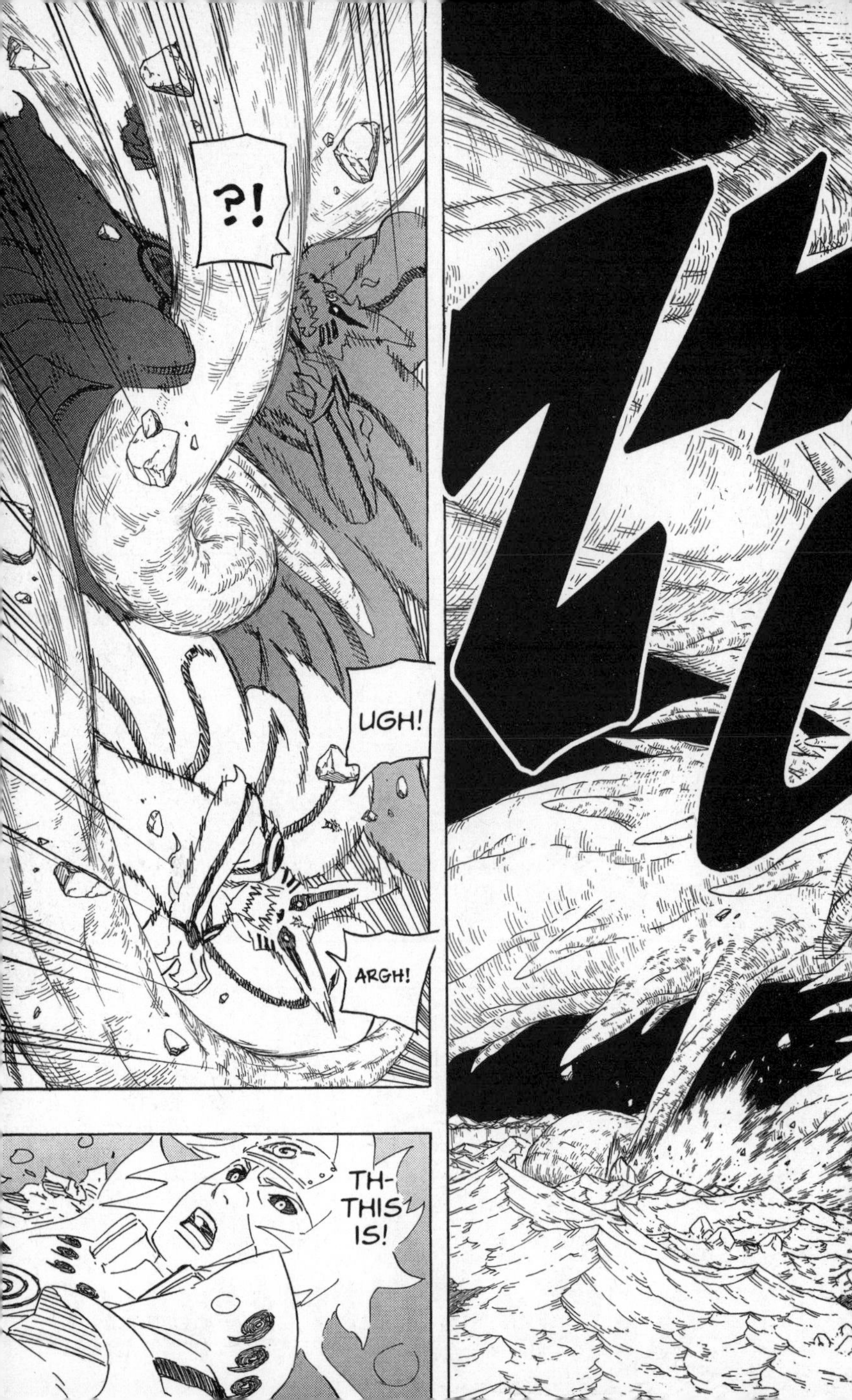
?!
UGH!
ARGH!
TH- THIS IS!

ZDTHD-THD-THD-
AARGH!!
WHOA!!
SHRRRRRRRRRRRL
?!!
?!!
?!
AAAR...
GUH...
ZWWWWWWWWWW...

GAH! IT SUCKS ALL YOUR CHAKRA IN ONE SWOOP!!!
RUN, OR YOU'RE DEAD!!
HELP!
A-A-RE YOU FREAKIN' SERIOUS?!
SHREE
IT'S GOING AFTER ALL OF US, ONE BY ONE!
WHY DO I GET SO MANY COMING AT ME, EH, FOOL, YA FOOL?!!
TAK
THIS IS THE DIVINE TREE!
TEN TAILS' FINAL FORM!!!
IT KNOWS THAT YOU HAVE MORE CHAKRA THAN MOST OF THE OTHERS.

AT THIS RATE, THE CHAKRA NARUTO SHARED WITH EVERYONE IS MEANINGLESS!!

UGH!!
THD-THD-
WH-WHAT EXACTLY IS IT?!!
THD-THD-

CHAKRA FIRST ORIGINATED WITH THIS DIVINE TREE!
ALL OF THE CHAKRA HERE, EVEN YOUR OWN VAST CHAKRA.

...
WHAT?

IT'S WE HUMANS WHO STOLE CHAKRA FROM THE DIVINE TREE LONG AGO.
THIS THING'S JUST TRYING TO GET IT BACK, THAT'S ALL.
W
W
ZW
W

ZWP

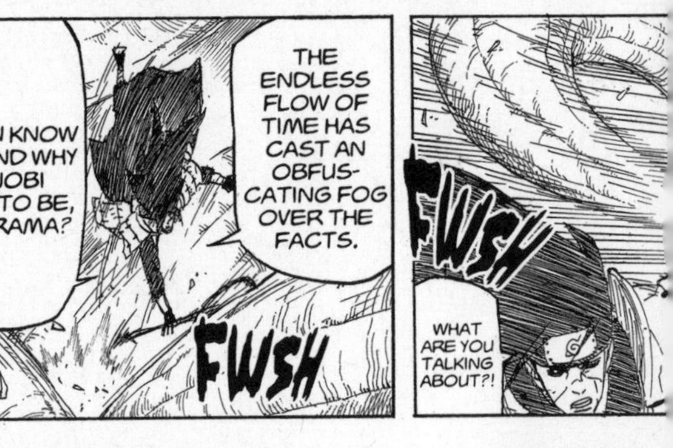

WHAT ARE YOU TALKING ABOUT?!
FWSH
THE ENDLESS FLOW OF TIME HAS CAST AN OBFUS-CATING FOG OVER THE FACTS.
FWSH
DO YOU KNOW HOW AND WHY SHINOBI CAME TO BE, HASHIRAMA?

?!

LONG, LONG AGO, BEFORE THEY EVEN HAD A CONCEPT OF CHAKRA...
...PEOPLE STILL CONTINUOUSLY BATTLED EACH OTHER.

THE DIVINE TREE, WITH NO INVOLVEMENT IN SUCH CONFLICTS...

...WAS WORSHIPPED BY THE MASSES AS A SACRED PILLAR.

AND THEN ONE DAY, THE TREE BORE A FRUIT THAT WAS SAID TO BE PRODUCED ONLY ONCE A MILLENNIUM.

I DON'T KNOW WHAT IF ANY SIGNIFICANCE IT HOLDS...

...BUT ACCORDING TO LEGEND THAT FRUIT WAS NEVER TO BE TOUCHED.

AND YET, THERE EMERGED A PRINCESS WHO TOOK AND TASTED...
...OF THAT FRUIT IN ORDER TO REAP THE TREE'S POWER AND WIN HER WAR.
HER NAME WAS OHTSUTSUKI KAGUYA.
AFTER-WARDS, KAGUYA GAINED THE POWER OF A GOD...
...AND WAS SAID TO HAVE QUASHED THE WAR ALL BY HERSELF.
SHE WAS THE VERY FIRST PERSON TO EVER HAVE CHAKRA...
...AND KAGUYA'S CHILD WAS BORN WITH CHAKRA ALREADY DWELLING WITHIN HIM.
HOWEVER, THE DIVINE TREE CAME ALIVE AND STARTED RUNNING AMOK, IN ORDER TO RECLAIM ITS STOLEN CHAKRA.
THAT IS TEN TAILS.
AND THE ONE WHO STOPPED IT WAS KAGUYA'S CHILD.
HIS NAME WAS OHTSUTSUKI HAGOROMO, AND HE IS THE FOREFATHER WHO PREACHED THE TEACHINGS OF CHAKRA AND BEGAN THE SECT OF SHINOBI...

THE MAN KNOWN AS THE SAGE OF SIX PATHS.

!
BUT HOW DO YOU KNOW SUCH THINGS?!
THO-THO-
THO-THO-

IT IS SO WRITTEN ON THE UCHIHA STONE TABLET.

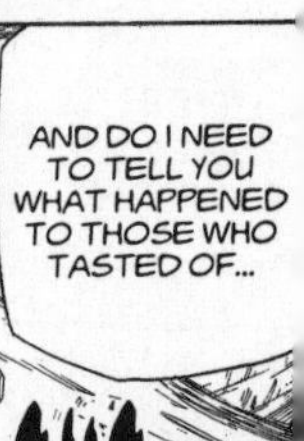

AND DO I NEED TO TELL YOU WHAT HAPPENED TO THOSE WHO TASTED OF...
THK-GUG-GUG-

...THE FORBIDDEN FRUIT FOR THE PURPOSE OF ENDING CONFLICT?

...

THAT'S RIGHT. NOTHING CHANGED.
IN FACT, SUBSEQUENT WARS BECAME EVEN MORE GRUESOME.

I DESPAIRED UPON LEARNING ALL OF THIS.
THERE ARE NO SUCH THINGS AS ***TRUE DREAMS*** IN THIS WORLD, HASHIRAMA!

FROM THE TIME PEOPLE TASTED OF THE FRUIT...
...HUMANS HAVE BEEN CURSED...
...AND DESTINED TO HATE EACH OTHER EVEN MORE!

AND IT IS WE SHINOBI WHOSE VERY EXISTENCE SYMBOLIZES THAT FOOLISHNESS, DON'T YOU THINK?!

IN WHICH CASE, I'D RATHER...

SO RELYING ON THE POWER OF THE DIVINE TREE AGAIN BY USING A GREAT GENJUTSU...

YOU JUST CAN'T SEE IT, WHAT'S EVEN FURTHER AHEAD...

IS THAT WHAT YOU MEANT BY "DREAMS OF THE FAR FUTURE"?!

...

TAK

tHK

BUT ONE THING IS OFF...
?
WHEN THIS DIVINE TREE BUD BLOSSOMS...

...THE EYE AT THE FLOWER'S CENTER WILL BE REFLECTED BY THE MOON...

...AND THE INFINITE TSUKUYOMI WILL BE FULLY ACTIVATED.
BUT THE ONE...

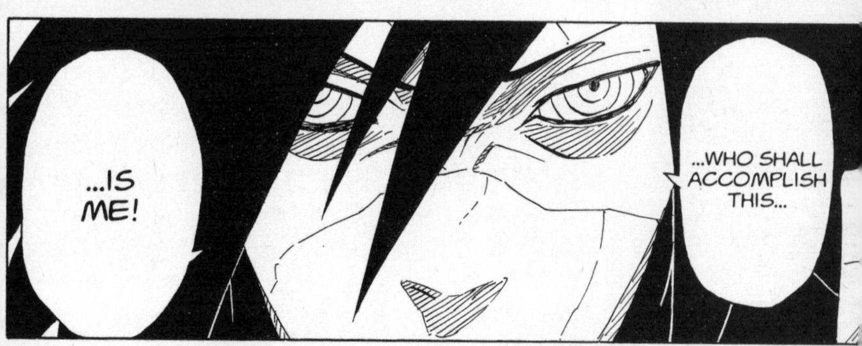

...WHO SHALL ACCOMPLISH THIS...
...IS ME!

ZHOOOOSH
WAH!!
!!
NARUTO!!!
FWP

WATER STYLE, SEVERING WAVE!!
ZLASH-ZLASH
SPROUT SPROUT
GAH! THERE'S TOO MANY!
I MIGHT BE ABLE TO SENSE NARUTO, BUT IT'S USELESS!
FOURTH, CAN YOU TELEPORT DIRECTLY TO NARUTO'S SIDE?!
SORRY, NO! MY CHAKRA'S BEEN DRAINED BY THAT LAST FLYING RAIJIN AND THESE VINES!
FEH!
TAK
WSH...
ZWWWW

THWK

KRK KRK KRK KRK KRK

GRAMPS!

...

GRAB
TAK
TMP
GOOD!
TAP
TAP
LET'S TELEPORT AWAY!
HAVE THINGS FINALLY SETTLED DOWN?!
!
!
FFT
...

GRT
!!
...THIS...
CAN'T TAKE...
...ANY MORE...
UGH...
ARE YOU ALL RIGHT, SAKURA?
HUF...
HACK
NOW, BE STILL...

...YOU'VE ALL ENDURED PLENTY ALREADY.

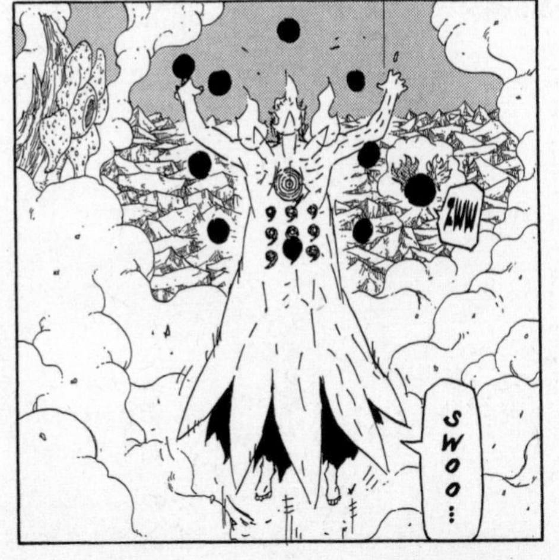
SWOO...
ZWM

Number 647: Regret

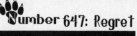

SHIKAMARU !!
HUFF
HACK

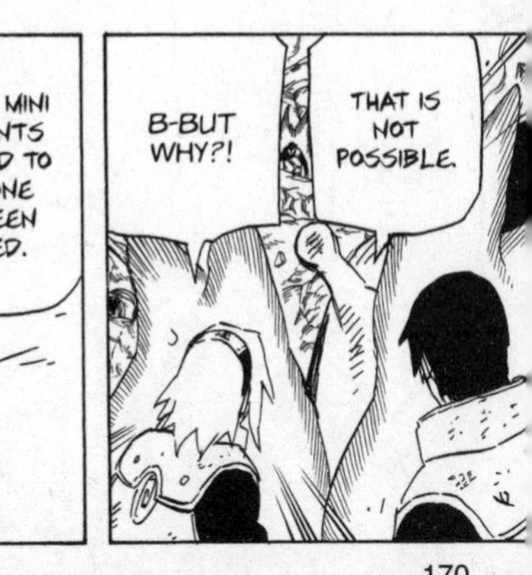

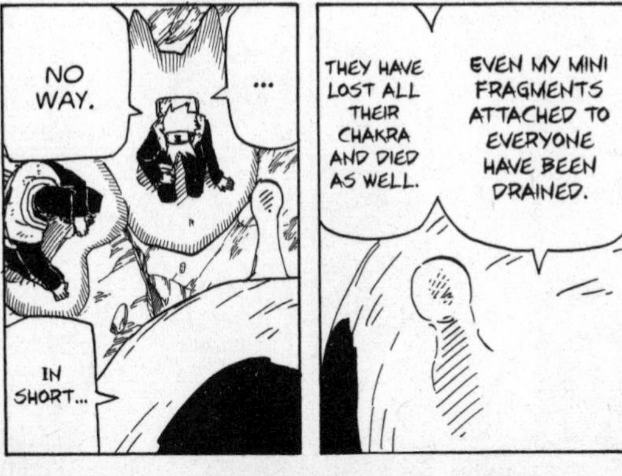

...EVERYONE IS IN THE SAME STATE AS MY FRAGMENTS.
SO SORRY... PA...
LOOKS LIKE I'LL... BE RIGHT ON YOUR HEELS...
TAK
SAKU-RA!
SHIKA-MARU !!
SORRY... MA...
IF WE'RE GONNA DIE ANYWAY...
...WE MIGHT AS WELL GO DOWN FIGHTING TO THE BEST OF OUR ABILITIES!!
BUT...
...AT THIS RATE...
TMP

...WE'LL ALL DIE BEFORE WE EVEN GET TO FIGHT!!

SHINOBI ARE DONE FOR. THERE'S NO NEED TO KEEP GOING.
IF YOU DON'T RESIST, I WON'T KILL YOU.

...
GNASH

GR...UGH.
AND IF YOU KEEP STANDING AGAINST US, YOU'LL CONTINUE TO LOSE YOUR COMRADES ONE BY ONE...
THIS SHALL BECOME A WORLD WHERE NO ONE WHO ACKNOWLEDGES YOU WILL EXIST...

UNLESS YOU WANT TO BE FILLED WITH REGRET...
...STOP AND DO NOTHING FROM HERE ON OUT.

YOU MEAN IF WE DON'T DO ANY-THING...
...WE'LL BE SAFE?

THAT'S RIGHT. YOU DON'T HAVE TO FEAR DEATH OR KEEP ENDURING ANY MORE PAIN.
YOU'LL BE ENTERING A DREAM.

DO NOT GIVE UP!!
IF YOU GET PUT UNDER GENJUTSU, YOU'LL BE THE SAME AS DEAD!!

...
...

THIS GIANT TREE IS INTIMATELY CONNECTED TO OBITO...
...LIKE AN EXTRA LIMB FOR EXTRACTING CHAKRA. WE CANNOT APPROACH IT CARELESSLY.

SUCH WORDS OF WEAKNESS.
SWSH
SO VERY UNLIKE YOU...

TWIP
...MASTER SARUTOBI.
SORRY TO KEEP YOU WAITING, JUGO!
SASUKE!

OROCHI-MARU, YOU'RE QUITE LATE!
AND THE GOKAGE?
I HAD THEM HEALED, SO AS LONG AS THEY DON'T CHICKEN OUT, THEY SHOULD BE COMING.
HMPH, STILL AS SARCASTIC AS EVER, EH.

YOU'VE COME.

...

HUH, THIS TREE REALLY *IS* HUGE, SEEING IT SO CLOSE UP.
I WONDER HOW LONG IT'LL TAKE TO CUT DOWN?
WHO CARES ABOUT THAT?
WHAT'S IMPOR-TANT RIGHT NOW...

...IS TO GO JUMP SASUKE AND LICK HIM ALL OVER, DAMN IT!!
QUIVER
QUIVER

...IS TO HEAL THE ALLIED FORCES SHINOBI, NO?
R-RIGHT! I KNOW THAT ALREADY, DAMN IT!

HE SEEMS TO BE IN A FOUL MOOD...

...
WHAT'S GOING ON...?

KEEN

SO WHEN'S *IT* GOING TO BLOOM?

EIGHT TAILS' AND NINE TAILS' JINCHURIKI ARE STILL ALIVE...
...GET IT?

SO EIGHT TAILS' AND NINE TAILS' CHAKRA...
...ARE ESSENTIAL FOR IT TO BLOOM AND COMPLETE THE JUTSU...

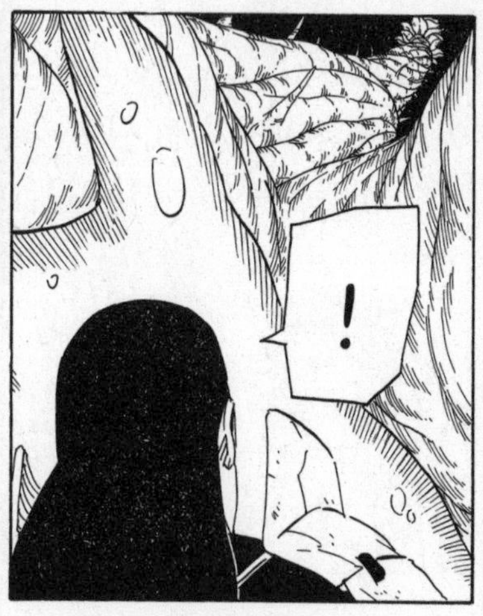
!

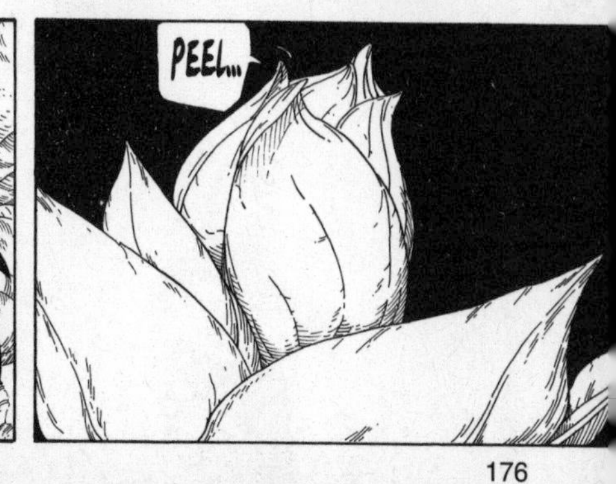
PEEL...

HOWEVER, IF IT CONTAINS EVEN A SMALL AMOUNT OF EACH OF THEIR CHAKRA, IT'S FINE.
IN SHORT, IT'S NOT LIKE IT *CANNOT* BLOOM.
ZWW...

ALL THAT IS AFFECTED IS **HOW LONG** IT'LL TAKE TO BLOOM.

THERE'S ABOUT 15 MINUTES TO GO...

IN THAT TIME, I SHALL STOP OBITO AND SWITCH PLACES WITH HIM...

...BY USING YOUR SAGE POWER.

...

THIS IS BAD. I MUST RELAY ALL THAT MY ORIGINAL BODY HAS HEARD TO THE REST OF THE ALLIED FORCES!

ARE THERE ANY OF THE YAMANAKA CLAN HERE?!

!

Y-YES, SIR!

DO YOU KNOW THE MIND TRANSMISSION TECHNIQUE?!

UH, YES, I DO, SIR!!

I ASK THAT YOU LINK ME TO EVERYONE HERE!

THERE ARE THINGS I'D LIKE TO EXPLAIN ABOUT THAT GIANT TREE AND THE INFINITE TSUKUYOMI!!

!!

THIS SENSATION...

!

GRAND-FATHER!!
AH! IS THAT YOU, TSUNA?!
THIS VOICE IS UNMISTAKABLY LORD HASHIRAMA'S!
I-IT MEANS THAT THE LORDS GOKAGE ARE CLOSE ENOUGH TO BE WITHIN RANGE OF MY JUTSU!

WHOOPS! THIS IS NOT THE TIME TO BE REMINISCING!
I HAVE THINGS I MUST RELAY TO YOU FIVE AND EVERYONE ELSE!

LISTEN CAREFULLY!!

AND YET, DOING NOTHING WILL YIELD THE SAME RESULT.

WE MUST EITHER CUT DOWN THAT TREE OR DEFEAT THE CASTER...

...WITHIN THE REMAINING TIME.

BUT...

DID I NOT
TELL YOU...
...NOT TO
GIVE UP?!!

...
...
...

...

...

...

SO YOU SAY, BUT YOU'RE AN EDOTENSEI, A PERSON FROM THE PAST...
...BROUGHT BACK TO LIFE!
WE ALL ARE STILL OF THE LIVING!

ZWW...
ZWW

THMP
...
IF THIS IS WHAT WAS TO BE, WE SHOULD'VE NEVER...
IT'S...
...OVER...
ZWW...

THAT'S RIGHT. JUST STAY LIKE THAT.
I'LL TAKE YOU TO A WORLD WHERE THERE ARE NO REGRETS.

GRR...
GR...

THOOM
THOOM

LET'S GO, JUGO.
SURE.

...
BLAZE

!!
!!

YOU THROWING IN THE TOWEL, NARUTO?
CUZ I'M NOT.

!
THESE ARE...

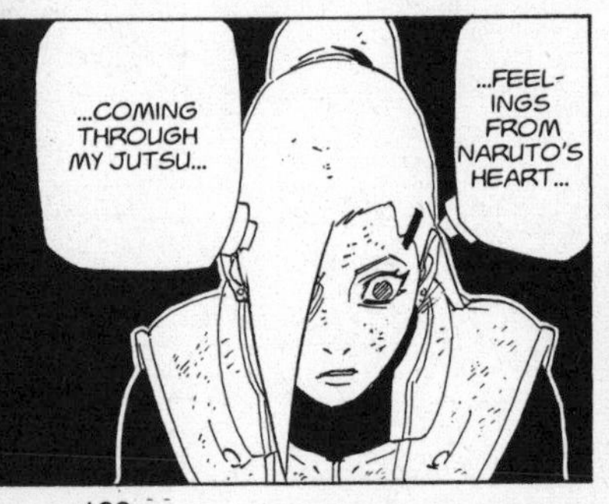
...FEEL-INGS FROM NARUTO'S HEART...
...COMING THROUGH MY JUTSU...

...

I KEPT THINKING...

...OVER AND OVER...
...BACK THEN, THAT I...

...SHOULD'VE CALLED OUT TO HIM.

...

HIS THOUGHTS ARE FLOWING IN...

THAT'S WHY...

忍
ワイワイ
ワイ

THESE ARE...
...

IT'S FROM THAT DAY...

...

猿飛 アスマ

...

...

...!...

...

...

...

...

...

...I DON'T WANNA REGRET ANYTHING!

...

I NEVER WANNA THINK, "I SHOULD'VE"!!

NARUTO!

WOOSH...

...
PLUS, I CAN'T JUST MAKE EVERYTHING...
TAK
...
...THAT WE'VE DONE UP TO THIS POINT MEANING-LESS!!

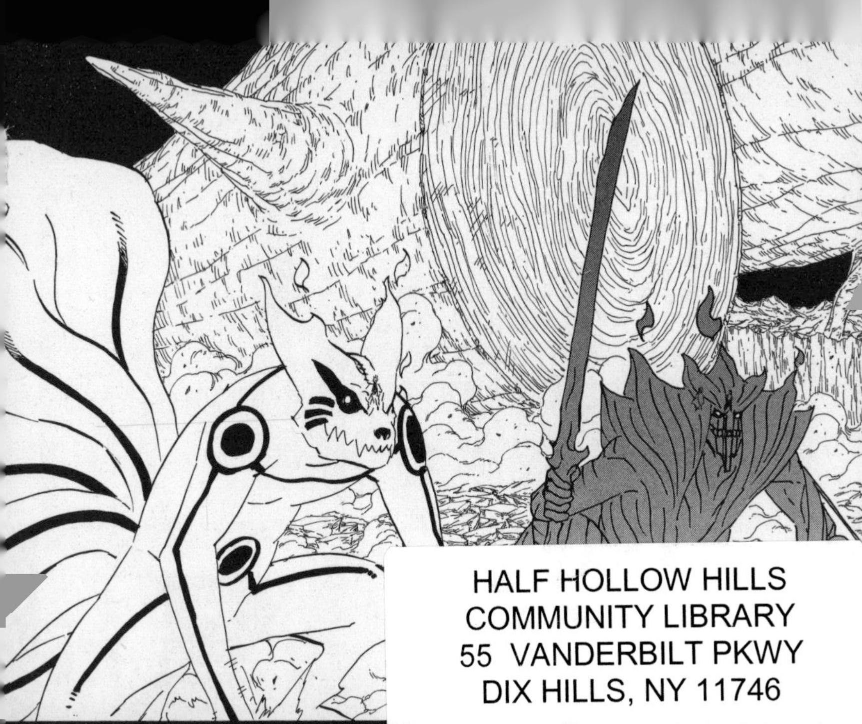

IN THE NEXT VOLUME...

PATH

As Obito tries to break the spirit of the Shinobi Alliance, Naruto stands strong as a symbol of inspiration to the others. With Sasuke's help, Naruto faces off against Obito, but his powers may be too much. Meanwhile, the Gokage and the rest of the alliance head toward the divine tree, but is it already too late...?

AVAILABLE DECEMBER 2014!

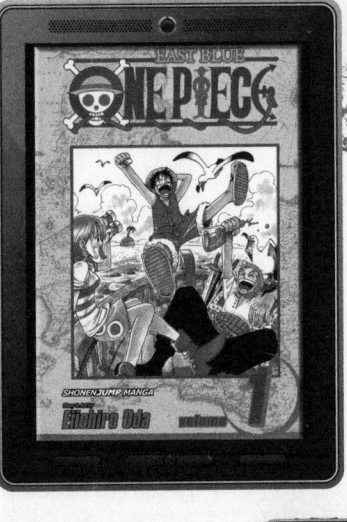

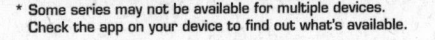

You're Reading in the Wrong Direction!!

Whoops! Guess what? You're starting at the wrong end of the comic!

...It's true! In keeping with the original Japanese format, **Naruto** is meant to be read from right to left, starting in the upper-right corner.

Unlike English, which is read from left to right, Japanese is read from right to left, meaning that action, sound effects and word-balloon order are completely reversed... something which can make readers unfamiliar with Japanese feel pretty backwards themselves. For this reason, manga or Japanese comics published in the U.S. in English have sometimes been published "flopped"—that is, printed in exact reverse order, as though seen from the other side of a mirror.

By flopping pages, U.S. publishers can avoid confusing readers, but the compromise is not without its downside. For one thing, a character in a flopped manga series who once wore in the original Japanese version a T-shirt emblazoned with "M A Y" (as in "the merry month of") now wears one which reads "Y A M"! Additionally, many manga creators in Japan are themselves unhappy with the process, as some feel the mirror-imaging of their art alters their original intentions.

We are proud to bring you Masashi Kishimoto's **Naruto** in the original unflopped format. For now, though, turn to the other side of the book and let the ninjutsu begin...!

—Editor

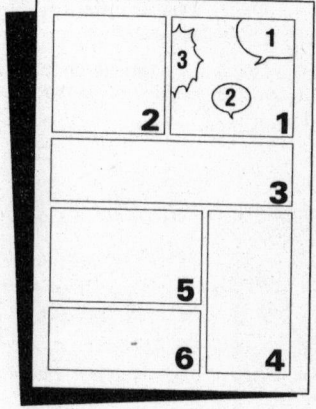